ARITHMETIC FOR BILLY GOATS

Arithmetic for Billy Goats

by Donald Barr

ILLUSTRATED BY DON MADDEN

Harcourt, Brace & World, Inc.

NEW YORK

CRB

Curriculum-Related Books, selected and edited by the School Department of Harcourt, Brace & World, are titles of general interest for individual reading, relevant to current school programs and courses.

 First edition. Library of Congress Catalog Card Number: 66-21608. Printed in the United States of America.

CHAPTER 1

CORNCOBS!

"Get those corncobs out of here!" yelled the Old Woman.

"Where can I put them?" asked the Old Man.

"Out of here, that's where you can put them! I'm sick and tired of corncobs, corncobs, corncobs, all over the place! Put them in the hilltop field and let the goats eat them!"

"That's a good idea," said the Old Man. "Goats like corncobs. I'll take them up there tomorrow."

"You'll take them up there right this minute!" screamed the Old Woman. "You're an old goat yourself, with your corncobs. I'm not going to have this place messed up with your smelly corncobs, do you hear? Out of here! Out, before I lose my temper! Out!"

"May I keep one to make a new corncob pipe with?" asked the Old Man.

"Out!" hollered the Old Woman.

* * *

The Old Man loaded the corncobs on his ramshackle old truck and drove them up to the top of the hill and dumped them in the middle of the field.

There were two goats in the field, a heavy goat with a long dirty beard and a skinny goat with no beard. The goats looked thoughtfully at the pile of corncobs, and the Old Man looked thoughtfully at the goats.

"Well, that's that," said the Old Man to himself. "And a terrible waste of good corncobs, if you ask me." He picked out a fat corncob to make a new corncob pipe with, stuck it in his pocket, and climbed into the truck.

And as he drove away, he said to himself, "That's the last we'll hear about corncobs, anyway."

CHAPTER 2

THE skinny goat, whose name was William Gruff, trotted over to the pile of corncobs.

"Hey!" yelled the heavy goat. "Get away from my corncobs!"

"Your corncobs?" asked William, surprised. *"Your* corncobs? How do you know they're yours, Uncle Max?"

"Well," said Max, "you don't think the Old Man gave all those rich, mellow corncobs to a stupid little kid like you, do you?"

"Maybe he did," said William. "I didn't hear him say: 'Max Gruff, all those corncobs are for you. Take them. Take them and share them with your horrible stringy nephew William.' I didn't hear the Old Man say that."

"Well, *I* heard him say it," said Max loudly.

"All right, Uncle Max," said the young goat. "If that's what you heard him say, that's what we have to do. Take the corncobs and share them with your horrible stringy nephew William." Then he looked puzzled and said, "William?" Then he looked very surprised and said, "William! Why, he must have meant *me!*" Then he looked worried and said, "Do *you* think I'm horrible and stringy, Uncle Max?"

"You're *very* horrible and stringy," said Uncle Max.

* * *

"How shall we share the corncobs?" asked William.

"We must make piles of corncobs, one pile for you and one for me," his uncle replied. "My pile will be over there, under that big apple tree. Yours can be over *there,* under that little apple tree."

"That's a good idea, Uncle Max," said William. "Apples taste very good with corncobs."

The two goats started trotting back and forth, each carrying corncobs over to his pile. Each one worked as fast as he could, and after a while, Max said, "Slow down a little. You'll get too tired."

"I feel fine, Uncle," said William, and kept on trotting.

After a while longer, Max said, "Slow down a little. *I'm* getting tired."

"You really ought to rest, Uncle," said William, and kept on trotting.

After another while, Max puffed, "This isn't fair. You're younger than I am."

"I can't help it, Uncle," said William. "I'm getting older as fast as I can." He kept on trotting.

"Wait a minute. Stop! I have an idea," gasped Max. "I'll carry corncobs to *your* pile and you carry corncobs to *my* pile."

"That's fair," said William.

The two goats began to carry corncobs again. But now Uncle Max trotted very slowly.

"I'm too old for this work," he explained. "I can hardly walk any more."

"I'm tired myself, all of a sudden," said William. "I must be getting older."

The two goats walked more and more slowly. Finally, Max said, "I think I'll rest awhile. You keep working. You're younger."

"I'll keep you company," said William.

The two goats rested and thought.

"Uncle Max," said William at last. "Now *I* have an idea. You move your pile over to the oak tree, and I'll move mine over to the pine tree. But this time, we'll do

it a different way. Each time you take one corncob to your pile, I'll take one over to my pile. Then the piles

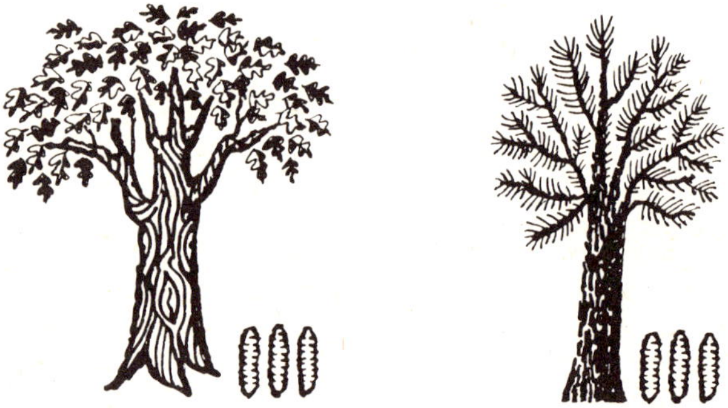

will always be just the same size as each other. And then we can walk just as slowly as we like and we can even stop and rest whenever we like."

"That sounds fair," said Uncle Max.

But when the job was done, the old goat stood in the middle of the field looking from the pile under the oak tree to the pile under the pine tree, and he said, "My pile looks smaller than yours."

CHAPTER 3

THE young goat looked at his uncle. He looked at the heaps of corncobs. The heaps looked alike. He looked at his uncle again. "Your pile looks smaller?" he asked.

"Smaller," said old Max.

"That pile there? The one under the oak tree?"

"Much smaller," said Max.

"I think the pile under the pine tree looks smaller," said William. "Let me look again, to make sure." He looked. "Yes, I was right. *My* pile is smaller. The one under the pine tree."

"*My* pile is smaller," said the old goat loudly, and he put his head down so that his horns stuck out in front of him.

The young goat stepped backwards carefully and asked, "Uncle Max, couldn't *both* piles be smaller?"

"No!" said Max.

"I didn't think so," said William. "Oh, well. Shall we do it all over again? Shall we make new piles?"

"No!!" said Max.

"All right," said William, meekly, "but we can do it all over again *in our heads*. Let's think about what we did."

He trotted in a circle around his uncle, thinking.

Then he came to a stop and asked, "Uncle Max, are you sure you put a corncob in your pile every time I put one in my pile?"

"Of course I did," said Max. "Do you think I'm stupid?"

William opened his mouth to answer the question, but then he quickly closed it again and trotted off in another circle around the old goat, thinking some more.

Then he stopped and said, "Uncle Max, I put a corncob in my pile every time you put one in your pile."

"Well, *good* for *you!*" said old Max nastily.

William started trotting in a circle again. "Every uncle-corncob has one nephew-corncob," he said as he went around. "And every nephew-corncob has one uncle-corncob. You could put every uncle-corncob next to his nephew-corncob—"

"Don't you touch those uncle-corncobs!" called out Max.

"I'm only doing it in my head," explained William.

"Don't even touch them in your head," grumbled his uncle. "I don't trust you."

But the young goat kept circling and thinking. "Suppose you did that, and suppose Uncle Max's pile *was* smaller—"

"It is," called out Uncle Max.

"—then there wouldn't be enough uncle-corncobs. There would be nephew-corncobs left over. But . . . there aren't. Well, suppose *my* pile was smaller—"

"It isn't," called out Uncle Max.

"—then there wouldn't be enough nephew-corncobs, and there would be uncle-corncobs left over. But . . . there aren't. One uncle-corncob to one nephew-corncob. One to one. One to one, one to one, one to one." Then William stopped trotting and walked over to the older goat. "Uncle Max," he said sadly, "we're both wrong. The piles are the same. One to one. The same."

"No, mine is smaller," said Max. "And what's worse," he added, "yours is bigger. And don't you start going around in circles again, you cheady greeter—I mean, you greedy cheater! You're making me dizzy!" He closed his eyes.

"All right, Uncle," said William. "Then you can have the pile under the pine tree and I'll take the one under the oak tree."

Uncle Max opened his eyes and looked for a long time at the piles of corncobs. "No," he said sulkily, "it doesn't matter." He yawned. "I'm tired. I think I'll go to sleep."

"So will I," said William. "Thinking is hard work too."

CHAPTER 4

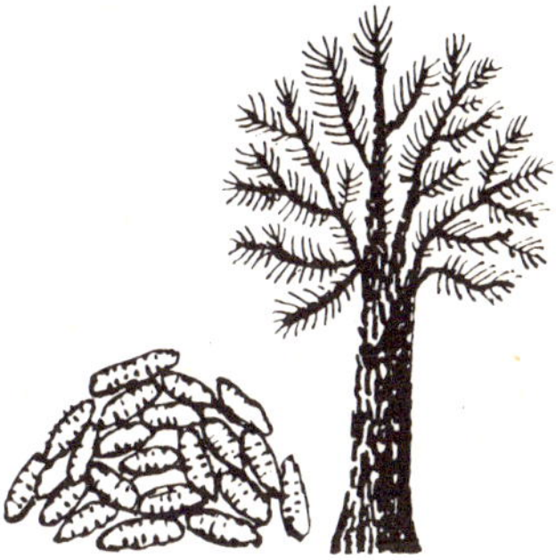

AS soon as William Gruff woke up the next morning, he trotted happily across the field to choose a corncob for breakfast.

Halfway across the field, he stopped.

He stared at the heaps.

Yes, he was sure of it.

The pile under the pine tree—*his* pile—was smaller than the pile under the oak tree—his uncle's pile.

William turned around and looked at Uncle Max. The old goat was asleep, snoring noisily. He looked very contented.

He also looked very fat.

William walked over to his uncle. "Uncle Max," he said into the old goat's ear. "Wake up, Uncle Max."

Max snorted and woke up. "Who's that? Oh, it's William. It *would* be." He grew angry. "How dare you wake me up!" Then he looked as if he had just remembered something. He grew friendly. "What do you want, young William?" he asked.

"Uncle Max, I've been thinking," said William. "Why don't you take the pile under the pine tree and I'll take the pile under the oak tree?"

"No! Certainly not! Never!" roared Max.

"But yesterday you said it didn't matter," said William.

"How dare you wake me up!" bellowed Max. "Go away and let me sleep!" He shut his eyes and began to snore loudly.

"Uncle Max," called William.

The old goat snored louder than ever.

The young goat looked from one heap to the other.

Yesterday, they had looked the same. One to one. He was sure of that.

While he was sleeping, some corncobs had left the pile under the pine tree. He was fairly sure of that.

Uncle Max was snoring away with all his might. His round belly rose and fell and quivered and shivered. William looked at it. It was wonderfully round. Never before had that belly been so round. William was almost sure of that.

He was angry, but he kept on thinking. The more he thought, the angrier he got; but the angrier he got, the harder he thought.

He said to himself, "If only I could carry all those corncobs out into the field . . . oh, those lovely mellow corncobs! . . . and lay them down side by side . . . how ripe they are! . . . one from the oak tree next to one from the pine tree . . . one from the oak, one from the pine . . . one to one . . . one to one, one to one, one to one . . . how rich they smell! . . . at last there would be no more corncobs under the pine tree . . . oh, that wicked old Max! . . . but there would be some corncobs left under the oak tree . . . *and I would eat them!*"

Then he said to himself, "But I can't carry all those corncobs out into the field, because Uncle Max is only making believe he's asleep, and he'll make believe he's waking up, and he'll *really* butt me with his wicked old horns."

And then William Gruff had a great idea.

He said to himself, "I could get some *other* things . . . they don't have to be corncobs . . . and I could take these other-things over to the pine tree and put them side by side with my corncobs . . . my delicious corncobs! . . . *one corncob* to *one other-thing* . . . *one to one, one to one* . . . until there were no more corncobs . . . and I would take all the other-things that were *not*

next to corncobs, and I would throw those away . . . and *then* I could take all the other-things that *had* been next to my corncobs . . . and carry them over to the oak tree . . . and put them next to Uncle Max's corncobs . . . one to one, one to one, one to one, one to one . . . until there were no more of the other-things, but there *would* be some corncobs left . . . AND I WOULD EAT THEM!"

Then he asked himself, "What shall I use for my other-things?"

*   *   *

And he answered himself, "Hoofs. I carry *them* around all the time."

He trotted over to the pine tree. He rolled a corncob off the pile, and he put one front hoof next to it. He rolled another corncob off the pile, and he put his other front hoof next to it. With his nose, he rolled another corncob off the pile, and he put one back hoof next to it. With his nose, he rolled another corncob off the pile, and he put his other back hoof . . . no, he didn't—he fell down.

"Hoofs don't work," he said. "Not enough hoofs."

He got up. "I need some other-things that I can get *lots and lots* of," he said. "Like . . . pebbles."

He scampered around the field, picking up pebbles with his teeth and carrying them to the pine tree. At last he had a fine big pile of pebbles there.

He placed a corncob next to a pebble, and another corncob next to another pebble . . . *one to one, one to one* . . . until all the corncobs had pebbles next to them. There were some pebbles he had not used. He kicked them away.

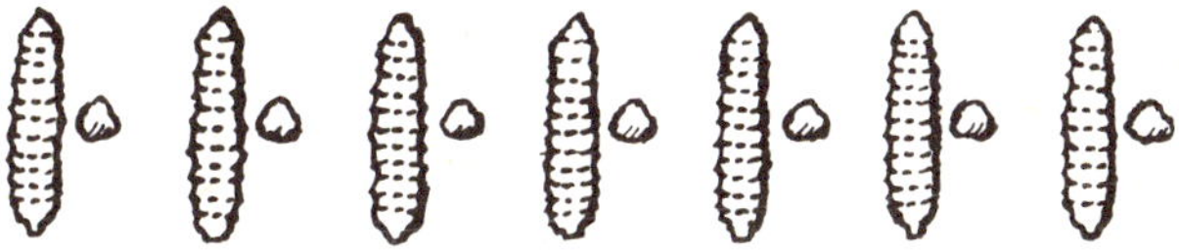

With his teeth, he picked up a pebble next to a corncob, then another, and another and another . . . until he had a mouthful of pebbles. He carried them over to the oak tree.

Uncle Max opened one eye. He kept on snoring. He watched William.

* * *

William went back to the pine tree and picked up another mouthful of pebbles. He was trotting happily over to the oak tree with them, when

gha-gha-*glmmpp!*

he swallowed a pebble.

Or was it more than one pebble?

Uncle Max laughed and then quickly shut his eye and snored even louder than ever.

CHAPTER 5

WILLIAM spat out the rest of the pebbles and trotted unhappily out into the middle of the field to think.

"Pebbles don't work," he said. "They hurt your throat."

And then William Gruff had another great idea.

He asked himself, "But why use *real* pebbles?" It was a good question. It was a powerful question. So he asked it again. "Yes, *why* use real pebbles?"

And he answered himself, "I shall *think* of some pebbles, and I shall carry them around in my head, not in my mouth."

He stood in the middle of the field and tried to think of pebbles.

It was very hard to do. It was easy to think of the pebbles, but all the pebbles he thought of looked alike. He kept forgetting them. He kept getting them mixed up.

"I must give them names," he said at last.

He trotted over to the pine tree and looked at a corncob on the ground. Then he *thought* of a pebble lying next to it and said, "Charley."

He looked at another corncob. He thought of another pebble. He said, "Jim."

He looked at corncobs and thought of pebbles, one to one, saying, "Danny. Bert. Bob. Irving. Wally. Sam. Henry. Mark. Joe."

When he had finished looking at all his corncobs, one by one, and thinking of pebbles with names, one to one, he went over to the oak tree.

He looked at a corncob and thought of the pebble named Charley. Another corncob and the pebble named Jim.

Corncob, and Danny the Pebble. Corncob, Bob the Pebble. Corncob, Irving the Pebble.

Wait a minute! There should have been a Bert in there. Had he used good old Bert? He was nearly sure he had *not* used Bert. All right: corncob, Bert the Pebble.

Now, where was he? He had just used Irving. Or was it Wally?

"Pebbles with names don't work," said William. "Too many names to remember."

* * *

"Hey, you!" yelled Uncle Max suddenly from his corner of the field.

William jumped.

"You get your hoofs off my corncobs!" roared Uncle Max.

"I–I'm not touching them, Uncle. Just thinking about them," said William.

"Well, get your thoughts off them," bellowed the old goat. "*Nobody* is going to think about my corncobs but *me*."

The young goat did not even hear him. William Gruff was staring down at his front hoofs. He had *almost* had his greatest idea.

CHAPTER 6

HE almost *had* it.

"The trouble is," he muttered, "when I used hoofs, I didn't have enough hoofs. When I used pebbles, I had too many pebbles. I didn't have enough hoofs to go with all the corncobs. I had too many pebbles to remember."

Over in his corner of the field, old Max puffed and grunted and heaved himself up on his four legs.

William did not see him. He was saying to himself, "If I use my hoofs over and over again, I'll have enough hoofs."

Old Max walked heavily across the field to his nephew.

William did not see him. He was saying to himself, "I don't need pebbles. I just need their names."

Old Max put his mouth next to William's right ear.

William did not see him. He was saying to himself, "I need lots and lots of names. But I can't remember lots and lots of names."

"Get out of here!" roared old Max. He roared it so loud that it sounded like *"Gerrahhah!"*

William did not hear him. He was saying to himself, "I could make pictures to help me remember."

Old Max walked out into the middle of the field. He looked at young William. He put his head down so that his horns stuck out in front of him. He rocked back and forth on his legs.

William did not see him. He was saying to himself, "I could make pictures to help me remember."

Old Max charged. His hoofs pounded the field. His big body moved faster and faster. His horns stuck out in front of him.

William did not see him. He was saying to himself, "I could make pictures to help me remember. *And I know how!"* And he marched off to the pine tree.

Old Max pounded right across the place where William had been standing. But William was not standing there. Old Max pounded into the pile of corncobs. The corncobs flew in all directions. Old Max's hoofs flew after them. Old Max's head hit the oak tree with a loud *thunk*.

William went to the pine tree and began to try out his new invention.

CHAPTER 7

WILLIAM Gruff, the Great Inventor, chose a flat place on the ground. He ate the grass from it. He scraped away the grass-roots with his hoofs. He now had a place for his pictures.

"I will start by making a picture of *no corncobs,*" he said.

He looked at the empty dusty flat place on the ground.

"That's a good picture of *no corncobs,*" he said. "But somebody might think it was *no picture*. I'll put a border around it."

So he scraped a circle in the ground. "That's nothing-with-a-ring-around-it," he said proudly. "It's a picture of

no corncobs, and its name is 'NO.' " He rubbed the circle away and blew the dust flat.

He rolled a corncob over. He put his right front hoof next to it.

"One corncob," he said. "One hoof. *One to one.*"

Then he went over and scraped a line in the ground.

"That's a picture of a corncob," he said. "Its name is 'YES.' " He rubbed the line away and blew the dust flat.

He rolled another corncob over next to the first one, and he put his right front hoof next to one corncob and his left front hoof next to the other.

"Now I've used up my front hoofs," he said. "Corncob, hoof. Corncob, hoof. *One to one.*"

He went over to the dusty flat place. "I want to make a picture to show that I used up my front hoofs *one time.* I'll make a YES."

He thought. "The trouble is," he said, "the last time I made a YES, it meant *one*-corncob-hoof. But I want this YES to mean both-hoofs-*one*-time. So I'll have to make this YES look a little different.

"Wait a minute!" he said. "I'd better not do that!" he said. "Because if I have different kinds of YESes, I'll get them all mixed up, the way I got the different pebbles named Charley, Jim, and Bert all mixed up.

"*What* shall I do? What *shall* I do? What shall I *do? I* know," he said: "I'll draw the same kind of YES, but I'll draw it in a different *place.*"

And he drew it a little ways over to the left side.

He looked at it awhile. He shook his head. "It *still* looks just like a picture of one-corncob-hoof. I have to show that it's in a different place. I'll put something in the place for one-corncob-hoof. What shall I put?"

He thought awhile. "I'll put a NO there. That means I used up my front hoofs *one* time and had *no* corncobs left over. That's what YES-NO means: YES, I used up both hoofs. NO, I didn't have any more corncobs." He drew it.

"The tricky thing about this," said William to himself, "is that NO always means no-corncobs, but YES means different things. When I put a YES *there*—" (and he pointed to the place on the right-hoof side) "—it means one-corncob-hoof. But when I put a YES *there*—" (and he pointed to the plane on the left-hoof side) "—it means one-corncob-hoof-*and*-another-corncob-hoof. That's funny! But I think it will get easier in a minute."

He rubbed the picture away and blew the dust flat.

* * *

He rolled another corncob over. He put his right front hoof next to one corncob and his left front hoof next to another, but there still was a corncob left over. He pulled back his hoofs and then put one of them next to the last corncob.

"This YES in this place means I used both my front hoofs one time," said William, scraping a line in the both-hoofs-one-time place. "And *this* YES in *this* place means there was one corncob left over and I had to use one hoof over again." And he started to scrape a line in the one-corncob-hoof place.

"What do you think *you're* doing?" said a voice in his ear.

"Oh, good morning, Uncle Max," said William. He

carefully finished scraping his line and then said politely, "I hope you slept well."

"No, I didn't," said Max.

"Why, what was wrong?" asked William. "Tummy-ache?"

"Nothing was wrong," said Max quickly. "Why does something have to be wrong? I can sleep badly if I want to. What are you doing there?"

"This is my invention," explained William proudly.

"What, that dusty place?" asked Max. "You call that an invention? Why, I've made bigger dusty places than that just eating my lunch!"

"Not the dusty place, Uncle. The pictures," said William.

"Where? Where? What pictures?" said the old goat, looking all around.

"Here," said William. "This is a picture of those corn-cobs."

Uncle Max looked at the lines William had scraped in the ground. "These holes in the ground?" he asked.

"Yes," said William.

"Pictures?" asked Uncle Max.

"Yes," said William.

"Of those corncobs?" asked Uncle Max.

"Yes," said William.

"Young William," said Uncle Max, "you are a very very dumb goat. Do you know what your pictures look like?"

"What?" asked William.

"Like holes in the ground. Not like corncobs," said Max firmly. "And do you know what else is wrong with them?"

"What else?" asked William.

"There aren't enough of them," said Max. "See here." He took one of the corncobs and put it on top of one of the lines. He took another corncob and put it on the other line. "There," he said, "that takes care of those pictures. But *this* corncob is left over. There is no picture of it. It's extra." He ate it.

CHAPTER 8

UNCLE," asked William, "can you hear me?"

"Of course I can hear you," said the old goat crossly.

"I didn't know," said William in a humble voice. "I didn't think you could hear anything but chewing."

He rolled over some corncobs. "After you swallow," he said, "I'll explain my invention."

"Glmmpp. Go ahead," said old Max.

William moved the corncobs off the pictures, rubbed the lines away, and blew the dust flat.

"Etch-hetch-hetchoo!" said old Max. "Stupid kid. I ought to butt you one."

William said, "No corncobs." He drew an empty circle. He rubbed it away. Uncle Max moved aside. William blew the dust flat.

William chose a corncob. "One corncob," he said. He put one hoof next to it. "One hoof," he said. He scraped a line in the dust. "This is the one-hoof place," he said, "and I'm putting a YES-line in it."

"Is *that* all?" asked Uncle Max. "Some invention!"

William rubbed out the picture and blew the dust flat. He put another corncob in place. "Corncob and corncob," he said. "Hoof and hoof," he said, putting them next to the corncobs. "This is the both-hoofs place," he said, "and I'm putting a YES-line in it." He did. "This is the one-hoof place," he said, "and I'm

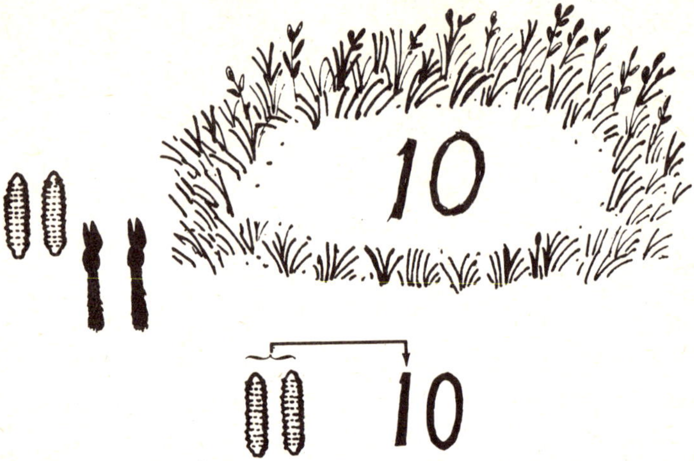

putting a NO-picture in it." He did. "YES-NO. YES, corncobs for both hoofs one time. NO other corncobs."

"You ought to make a line and another line, one for each corncob," said Max. "Easier to draw."

"Wait," said William. He put another corncob in place. "Corncob, corncob, corncob," he said. "Both hoofs. One hoof again. YES in the both-hoofs place. YES in the one-hoof place. YES-YES."

He rubbed the picture away, blew the dust flat, and put another corncob in place. "Corncob, corncob, corncob, corncob," he said. "Both hoofs. Both hoofs again. . . . Oh dear!"

"Thought you were so smart, didn't you?" said old Max helpfully.

"*I* know," said William Gruff. "I'll use *another* place. It will be the place where I can make a picture that shows whether I've used both front hoofs and then used them again."

"You're getting me mixed up," said old Max.

"It's not so hard to get *you* mixed up, Uncle," said William. "The trouble is, I'm getting *me* mixed up too."

He stared at the corncobs. Then he said, "I'm going to think of it this way: I'm going to use lots and lots of picture-places. I'm going to use all the places I need. I'm

going to start at the right-hoof side because . . . well, because I *did* start at the right-hoof side. Each picture-

1 and 1 are 10

place will be empty or full. It will be *empty* if there's a

10 and 1 are 11

NO there. It will be *full* if there's a YES there."

11 and 1 are 100

"What if there's a line there, and you get another corncob and you have to put another line there?" said Uncle Max. "It's full. You're stuck. This is a stupid game."

"It is not," said William. "I go to the next picture-place. I did that already. YES means one corncob. I wanted to put in another corncob, and so I wrote YES-NO. I emptied the right-hoof picture-place and put a YES in the next picture-place. YES and YES make YES-NO."

"That's the part I don't like," said Max.

"*That's* my invention," said William. "So if I have YES-NO corncobs and I want to put in YES-NO more corncobs, what happens? The place at the right-hoof end is empty, and I don't have to put anything in it. But the next place is full. There's a YES there. And I want to put

 and  are 

10 and 10 are ?

another YES there. So I empty that picture-place and I put a YES in the next place, and I have YES-NO-NO."

	0		1
and	0	and	1
are	0	are	10

So

	10
and	10
are	100

"It's a stupid game," said old Max.

"It's not a game, Uncle," said William. "You'll see."

William Gruff put another corncob in place. "I'm adding just plain YES to YES-NO-NO. So I put my new YES in the right-hoof place, which is empty. YES-NO-YES."

 and  are 

100 and 1 are 101

BECAUSE

	100
and	1
are	101

He put in another corncob. "This new YES wants to get into the right-hoof place. But it's full. There's a YES there already. So I empty the right-hoof place and fill the *next* place. YES-YES-NO."

 and  are 

101 and 1 are 110

BECAUSE

	101
and	1
are	110

He put in another corncob. "Now the right-hoof place is empty again. So I can put my new YES in it. YES-YES-YES."

 and  are 

110 and 1 are 111

BECAUSE

$$\begin{array}{rr} & 11\,|\,0 \\ \text{and} & 1 \\ \hline \text{are} & 11\,|\,1 \end{array}$$

He put in another corncob. "But now we're all full. I try to put my new YES in the right-hoof place. It's full. I empty it, and I try to put a YES in the next place. But

 and  are 

111 and 1 are 

it's full. So I empty it, and I try to put a YES in the *next* place. But *it's* full. So I empty it and start a new place. YES-NO-NO-NO."

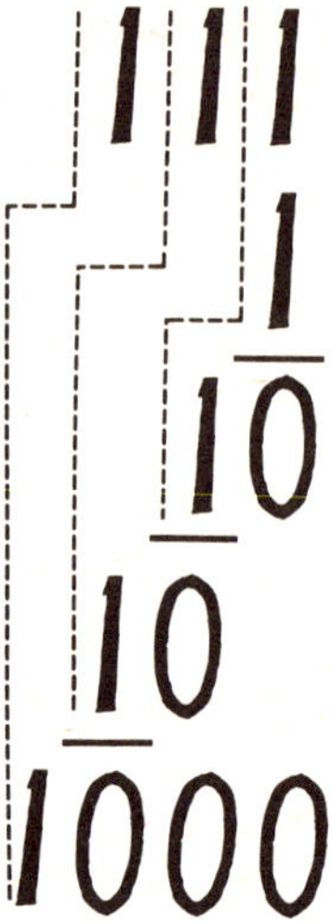

"If this isn't a game, what is it?" asked old Max.

"You'll see," said William. He went to get more corncobs.

One by one, he added to the row of corncobs next to the flat dusty place. YES by YES, he added to the pictures in the flat dusty place.

After a while, he got to YES-YES-YES-YES. Then he put another corncob in place, and he had YES-NO-NO-NO-NO.

 and 

are 

1111 and 1 are

10000

At last he got to YES-YES-YES-YES-YES.

"Uncle Max," he said.

Uncle Max had gone to sleep.

"Uncle Max," said William.

Uncle Max opened one eye. "Still playing that stupid game?" he asked.

"It's not a game," said William. "And I want you to help me. I've got YES-YES-YES-YES-YES here. I'm going to put in another corncob. That means I will need another picture-place. But I have no more room for pictures. Help me eat some of this grass, so I have more room."

"I'm not hungry," said Max.

"You're not hungry?" said William, very surprised. "You only had one corncob for breakfast—my corncob. And you're *not hungry?*"

Old Max looked sulky. "I'm not hungry, that's all. If I don't want to be hungry, I don't have to be hungry. Anyway," he added, "I have a stomach-ache."

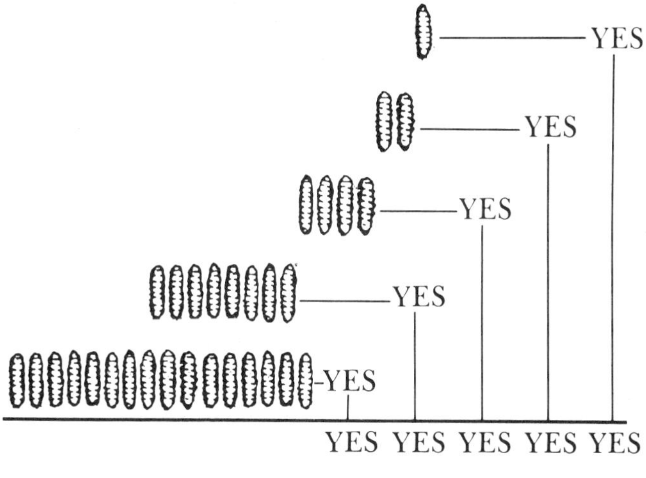

So William ate away the grass and scraped away the grass-roots and made some more room for picture-places.

And he put in another corncob, and he had YES-NO-NO-NO-NO-NO.

And after a while, he had YES-YES-YES-YES-YES-YES. And he put in another corncob, and he had YES-NO-NO-NO-NO-NO-NO.

And after a while, he had YES-YES-YES-YES-YES-YES-YES. And he put in another corncob, and he had YES-NO-NO-NO-NO-NO-NO-NO.

And after a while he had YES-YES-NO-NO-NO-YES-NO-YES. And there were no more corncobs under the pine tree.

"YES-YES-NO-NO-NO-YES-NO-YES," said William. "*YES*-YES-*NO*-NO-*NO*-YES-*NO*-YES, *BUT* IT'S *NOT* A GAME!" he sang, and did a little dance.

CHAPTER 9

THEN he said, "Uncle Max, I'm going to eat some grass over by the oak tree. Near your corncobs."

Old Max said, "Go ahead."

William said, "Grass is good for tummy-aches, Uncle."

Old Max said, "Not for this tummy-ache."

William went over to the oak tree and ate and scraped and made a large flat dusty place.

"Uncle Max," he called. "I'm going to make pictures of your corncobs."

"Oh, no you're not!" said old Max and scrambled up on his legs. "You leave those corncobs alone!" he said, trotting towards his nephew.

"All right, Uncle," said William, *"you* can make the pictures."

"No, I can't," said Max. "I—I can't see so well. Because of my stomach-ache," he explained.

"All right, Uncle," said William, "you put the corncobs out in nice straight rows, and I'll make the pictures."

"Why do you want to make pictures of my corncobs?" asked old Max.

"Just to see if I get YES-YES-NO-NO-NO-YES-NO-YES," explained William. "That's what I got for *my* corncobs."

"Of *course* you'll get YES-YES-whatever-it-is," said Max. "You said yourself that the piles were the same."

"But you said your pile was smaller," said William. "If your pile is smaller, I'll give you some of my corncobs."

"The piles are the same size," said old Max.

"Then what are you afraid of?" asked young William.

* * *

Uncle Max put the corncobs into neat rows. William made pictures, rubbed them out, blew the dust flat, and made more pictures, until he came to YES-YES-NO-NO-NO-NO-NO-NO.

Then a moment later he came to YES-YES-NO-NO-NO-NO-YES-YES.

Then he added a corncob and got YES-YES-NO-NO-NO-YES-NO-NO.

Then he added a corncob and got YES-YES-NO-NO-NO-YES-NO-YES.

And there still were a lot of corncobs under the oak tree.

"Uncle," said William Gruff, "what's wrong with my invention?"

"I—I don't know," said old Max.

"Uncle," said William Gruff, "what's wrong with your tummy?"

"I—I—I don't know," said old Max.

"But *I* know. *Nothing* is wrong with my invention. And *corncobs* are wrong with your stomach—*my* corncobs."

* * *

"Yesterday," said William Gruff the Great Inventor, "every uncle-corncob over here had a nephew-corncob over there." He pointed a hoof at the pine tree. "One to one," he said.

"Today," he said, "there are YES-YES-NO-NO-NO-YES-NO-YES nephew-corncobs over there." He pointed a hoof at the pine tree.

"And today, there are YES-YES-NO-NO-NO-YES-NO-YES uncle-corncobs right here." He pointed to the corncobs which Uncle Max had put out in straight rows. "*These* uncle-corncobs still have nephew-corncobs. One to one."

He pointed a hoof at the corncobs lying in a heap under the oak tree. "But today, *those* uncle-corncobs don't have

nephew-corncobs. *What happened to their nephews?*"

"I—I—I—I don't know," said Uncle Max.

"But *I* know," shouted William. "They sneaked into your tummy while you were asleep and gave you a tummy-ache!"

Uncle Max groaned.

"We have to be fair, Uncle Max," said William very softly. "We have to put their uncles into *my* tummy and give *me* a tummy-ache too."

And so William ate the corncobs left over under the oak tree.

And since he had also eaten a lot of grass to make room for his pictures, he got an even worse stomach-ache than Uncle Max had.

But William Gruff didn't care. He was happy. He had invented arithmetic.

WELL, now, that's a strange story. I don't believe it really happened.

And William Gruff's arithmetic is strange arithmetic. It certainly isn't the arithmetic I learned when I was a kid in school.

But that's because I was a human kid, not a young goat. I had ten fingers at the ends of my front limbs, instead of two hoofs. So the arithmetic I learned in school was ten-fingered arithmetic, instead of two-hoofed arithmetic. . . . I think I'd better explain the difference.

Humans invented arithmetic just about the way William Gruff did. They did it thousands and thousands of years ago, and they took thousands of years to do it. But their ideas were really the same.

First, they invented a question: "How many?"

That was a great invention, that question. The man who first thought of it had a wonderful brain. You have to remember: those people had never even heard of numbers, or counting, or *anything* like that. And then one day some great man looked at a pile of stones, or a bunch of grapes, or a herd of cows, and he suddenly saw that the pile or bunch or herd had an important *something* about it—something that wasn't stony, or grapey, or cowy—something that was . . .

But what *was* it?

He had no words to say it with, you see.

I suppose he said to himself: "Which bunch of grapes shall I pick, this one or that one?" And he liked grapes.

Or maybe he said to himself: "Here are Og's cows, and there are Ug's cows. Shall I marry Og's daughter, or shall I marry Ug's daughter?" And he wanted cows.

Well, whatever he said to himself, the question *How many grapes in that bunch?* or *How many cows in that herd?* got into his head at last.

Then people invented another great idea: "Equals."

After all, this herd of cows couldn't be *the same* as that herd of cows, because they weren't *the same* cows. So for a long time, nobody noticed that the question *How many cows in this herd?* could have the same answer as the question *How many cows in that herd?*

Come to think of it, the question *How many cows in this herd?* could have the same answer as the question

How many stones in this pile? Nowadays, we could say: "The number of cows in this herd EQUALS the number of stones in this pile." But in those days, people hadn't thought of numbers yet.

Somewhere, at some time, some thinker (just like William Gruff) said to himself: "Suppose I took a stone from this pile and put it next to a cow from that herd. And suppose I kept doing this. One stone, one cow. One to one.

And suppose, when it was all done, there was no stone without its cow, and no cow without its stone. I wouldn't know HOW MANY cows there were. I wouldn't know HOW MANY stones there were. But I *would* know that this herd and this pile had the same . . ."

The same *what?*

You see how close he was getting.

Then people invented counting. All they needed was a big bunch of names—names that they could remember. Instead of putting stones next to cows, one to one, they could put these names next to the cows, one to one.

And they were always careful to say the names the same way. They had to be, of course. Otherwise, the plan wouldn't work, as William Gruff found out. They chose a name to say first, and they always said that one first. They chose a name to say next, and they always said that one next. And they kept this up until every cow in the herd, or every grape in the bunch, had been named.

And this was a tremendous invention. Because now they had a simple way of answering the question *How many?*

The last name they used was the answer.

Suppose you named a flock of sheep: Oinos, Dwou, Trei, Quetwor, Pengkwe, Sweks, Septim, and Oktou. And suppose everyone knew these names, and everyone always said them in the same order. Then if somebody asked you, "How many sheep are there?" you might just say, "Oktou." Everyone would know that there were enough sheep to use up the names from Oinos to Oktou.

(I didn't make up these names. They were invented by a mysterious tribe of people who lived thousands and thousands and thousands of years ago in the northeastern part of what is now Europe. These names have been copied by all kinds of people ever since. The Hindus in ancient India, the Greeks in ancient Greece, the Romans in ancient Italy, the Germans, the Russians, the Irish— all these people copied their counting-names from that one tribe. Of course, after a long, long time, different people did begin to pronounce the words differently. But I want you to do something: I want you to say, "One, Two, Three, Four, Five, Six, Seven, Eight," while you look at Oinos, Dwou, and the rest. You see: we are still copying most of our counting-names from those old old names, even today.)

So now people had . . . *numbers.*

Numbers are not names. Numbers *have* names. (If we want to sound very mathematical, we call these names "numerals.") Suppose I own some cows. Here they are:

You ask me, "How many cows do you have?"

I want to answer you by telling you the *number* of cows I own. How shall I do this?

I point to one cow with one finger, to another cow with another finger, and the last cow with another finger. I then hold up the fingers. The fingers aren't a number. The *number* of fingers is the *number* of cows.

Or I could use names instead of fingers, and say, "One, Two, Three." The names aren't a number, but the *number* of names is the *number* of cows.

Or I could just say, "Three." You would know that "One" and "Two" came before "Three." They always do.

Or I could say, "Trois." (I'd pronounce it "Tr-wah.") That's another name for the number, a French name.

Or I could say, "Drei." (I'd pronounce it "Drhy.") That's another name for the number, a German name.

But it is hard to remember names. You could remember Oinos, Dwou, Trei, Quetwor and a few more: that's not hard. But sooner or later you would begin to get mixed up, just as William Gruff did at first.

In the days when numbers were first discovered and names for them were invented, people didn't write. They hadn't thought of it yet. And even if they *had* known how to write, it wouldn't have done any good to write the counting-names down—not unless everyone carried a long, long list of them around. Remember: the counting-names were no good unless everyone said the same names in the same way. Think of those poor savages stumbling through the forests carrying huge rolls of tree-bark or animal-skin covered with names, just in case they needed to count. . . . It was a problem.

It was a problem which many tribes never did solve. Years ago I met a man who had just come back from Africa. He told me that he had been living with a savage tribe that counted: One, Two, Three, Four, A Heap. Then they gave up. Anything more than four was "A Heap." Five was "A Heap." Five Hundred was "A Heap." (They used their own African words, of course. But I forget them.) If I went to Africa *now,* I couldn't find those savages any more. Now I would find everyone counting: One, Two, Three, Four, Five, Six, Seven, and so on. Or, more likely, I would find them counting: Un, Deux, Trois, Quatre, Cinq, Six, Sept, which is the same thing in French. Nearly everybody in the whole world has begun to use our system of counting.

Because, you see, the people who invented our system of counting did solve the problem—the problem of having enough names to count with but not having too many names to remember.

They did what William Gruff did. They made up just a few words and they thought up a simple way to use those words over and over.

William Gruff, who had two front hoofs, made up two

words: NO and YES. We humans, who have ten fingers on our front paws, made up ten words: ZERO, ONE, TWO, THREE, FOUR, FIVE, SIX, SEVEN, EIGHT, and NINE.

It wasn't easy. The hardest counting-word to invent was ZERO. It took many thousands of years to do it. After all, if you count on your fingers, what do you do? You put each finger next to something that's there, one to one. You don't think of putting one finger next to something that isn't there. So Zero took a long time to figure out.

William Gruff had a simple way of making up a lot of counting-names by using a few words over and over again. He made a row of words.

No, I'm wrong. That's not what he did. He made a row of *places* to put words. The words he used were No and Yes. The place at the right-hand end of the row was the doorway to the row. That's where numbers went in.

Let's watch them go in. Ready?

All the places are empty. Along comes our first number. What is it? Nothing. So we write its name:

That's the name of a number. Suppose you ask me, "How many cows do you own?" I can answer, "I own no cows."

Along comes another number. We call it by the name One. It goes in the door. It takes the place of No:

That's the name of a number. Yes in the doorway-place means One.

Along comes another One to make another number. It tries to go in the door. But that Yes is in the way. What shall we do?

Max Gruff told William Gruff to make the old Yes move over to the next place, and to put a new Yes in the doorway-place. But *you* know what would happen if we did that. We'd have a long parade of Ones coming along and pushing their way in and we'd end up with a huge long string of Yeses.

William Gruff had a better idea. He said that the Yes in the doorway-place stands for One. A new One has come along. The Yes will move over to the next place, *but now it will stand for both Ones.* And since nothing is left in the doorway-place, we'll put a No there:

This is the name of the number One-and-One, which we call by the numeral Two.

But now we notice something strange about that Yes. It used to mean One. Now it has moved over to the next place, and it means Two. Let's see what happens to it when some more numbers come in the door.

Here comes another One to make the number bigger.

That was easy. Its name, Yes, just took the place of the No in the doorway:

So that's the name of the number Two-and-One, which we call Three.

Notice: the new Yes in the doorway-place stands for One, and the old Yes in the next place still stands for Two.

Another One is on the way. Now there *will* be some pushing and shoving. . . . The new One tries to get in and bumps into the Yes in the doorway-place. They join together and go into the next place, where a Yes will stand for both of them. Oh! But there's a Yes there already. So they join with *that* Yes and go into the next place. And in that next place, Yes will stand for *all* of them. Meanwhile, there's nothing left in the places they've passed:

That's the name of the number Three-and-One, which we call Four.

Now we see what happens to a Yes every time it moves over another place. In the doorway-place, it meant One.

In the next place, it meant One-and-One, or Two. In the *next* place, it meant Two-and-Two, or Four. We can make a chart of what Yes is worth in each place:

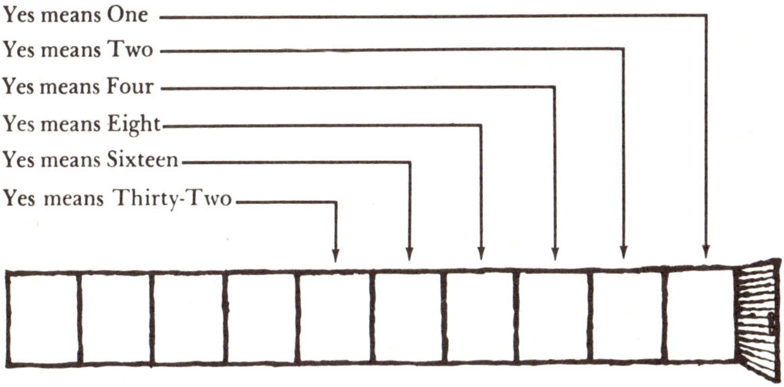

Perhaps you can figure out what Yes stands for in the other places.

So, by William Gruff's great invention, we can write the name of the number we call "Twenty-Nine" as

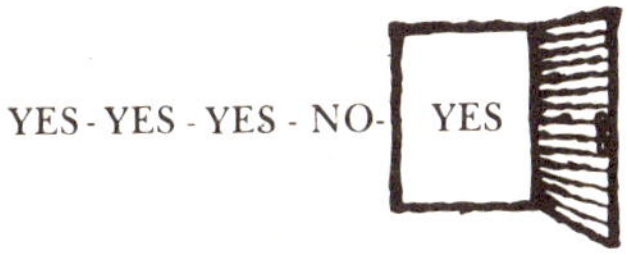

What we would call "Fifty-Four" William Gruff would call

Simple?

Simple!

Of course, billy goats can't write very well. So William Gruff wrote Yes down as 1, and he wrote No down as 0.

Our own ten-fingered way of making up counting-names uses the same rules, except that we have ten words, so it takes longer for our names to go from place to place.

We start with all the places empty. Then our first number, Nothing, comes along. It enters the door:

Along comes a One, and takes the Zero's place:

Another One comes and changes the old One to One-and-One, or

Another One changes the Two to Two-and-One, or

This keeps happening, and we have

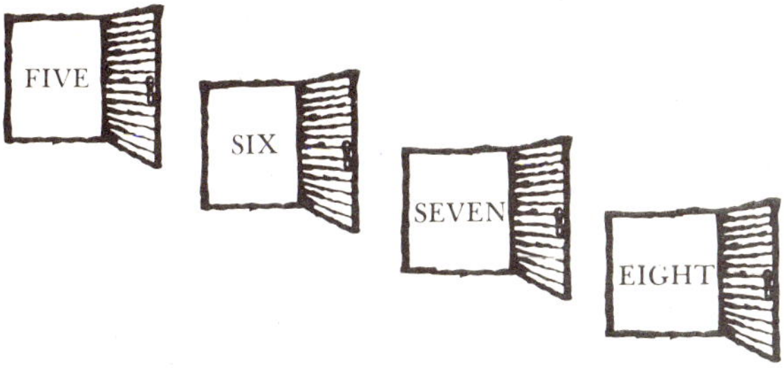

and

in the doorway-place, one after another. Then along comes another One. But we cannot have anything more than Nine in the doorway-place, so we start over again with a Zero in the doorway-place, and we begin putting words into the next place:

That's the name of a number which we have nicknamed "Ten."

But we notice something about the "One" in that name. It doesn't stand for One any more. Now that it has moved over a place, it stands for the number of fingers we have on our hands.

But Ones keep crowding into the doorway:

And this keeps happening until the word Nine is in the doorway-place:

And another One comes skipping up, and

That's the name of a number we call "Twenty." The Two in that name doesn't mean One-and-One. It really means Ten-and-Ten. So the place just next to the doorway-place is called the Tens Place. The doorway-place itself is called the Ones Place.

You know what the next place is called.

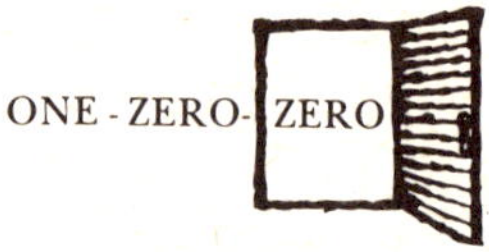

That's the name of a number we call "One Hundred." The place where the "One" is sitting is called the Hundreds Place, because that "One" doesn't mean One. It means the number of fingers that ten people should have on their hands.

Writing is a lot of work. So we often make our work easier by writing 0, 1, 2, 3, 4, 5, 6, 7, 8, and 9, instead of Zero, One, Two, Three, Four, Five, Six, Seven, Eight and Nine.

Simple?

Well–not *too* hard!

I think you could learn a lot by making a list of numbers using our counting-names and then putting William Gruff's counting-names next to them. Like this:

0	0
1	1
2	10
3	11
4	100
5	101

Try going all the way up to one hundred. When you've done that, look down the list of billy goat counting-names. Watch the right-hand places. They go 0, 1, 0, 1, 0, 1 . . . Then look at the next-to-the-right-hand places. How do they go? And the *next* places. How do they go? And the next and the next. How do they go? And why? (Let me help you make sure you got your lists right. Our 50 should be William Gruff's 110010. Our 100 should be William Gruff's 1100100.)

If you have been watching me very closely, you must have caught me cheating a little.

I've been sneakily using a trick we call *addition* without saying so. As a matter of fact, on page 62, I even used a trick we call *multiplication,* and I sort of covered it up.

So maybe I'd better go back to the time when people were just discovering these tricks.

Once people had invented counting-names, they began to discover all sorts of things.

Suppose they had two sets of corncobs:

 and 

They counted one set. They got Pengkwe, or 5. They counted the other set. They got Trei, or 3. Then they counted all the corncobs and they got Oktou, or 8. So they said that Pengkwe and Trei are Oktou, or $5 + 3 = 8$. They had discovered addition.

They also discovered that if they counted the same corncobs from the other end, they first got Trei and then Pengkwe, but they still had Oktou corncobs when they were all done. So $3 + 5 = 8$. So Pengkwe and Trei are the same as Trei and Pengkwe, or $5 + 3 = 3 + 5$. That was a useful thing to know about addition: if you add up the same numbers, you always get the same answer. It doesn't matter what order you add them in.

People are lazy. They are always looking for an easier way to do things. Counting corncobs one by one is all right when you only have a few corncobs. But suppose you have all these:

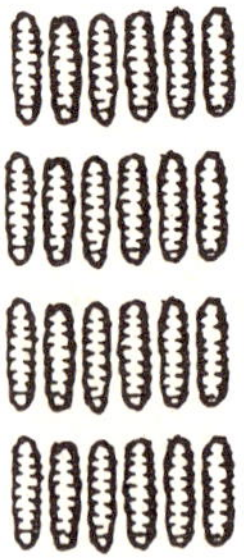

Then you have $6 + 6 + 6 + 6$ corncobs.

Thousands of years ago, some clever, lazy fellow was thinking about this, wishing he didn't have to count and count and count. Maybe he was an Egyptian. Maybe he was the Pharaoh's cook, and he had to figure out how much corn to boil when the Pharaoh gave a party. Maybe the Pharaoh always ate six ears of corn for dinner (although, to tell you the truth, I don't think Egyptians ate corn on the cob at all—but *suppose* they did), and of course his guests had to eat just what he ate. It was hard to boil up exactly the right number of ears of corn when the Pharaoh and 736 of his best friends were going to sit down to dinner. The Pharaoh didn't like to have corn left over. "Don't waste corn," he always said. It was one of his favorite sayings. But he didn't like to have his friends go hungry, either. "Be sure there's enough corn," he used to warn the cook. And maybe there was one day when the Pharaoh was going to have only three friends in for dinner . . . and the cook put four rows of corn on the table,

with six ears of corn in each row: He walked around the end of the table to get something, and he happened to look down at the corn, and he saw:

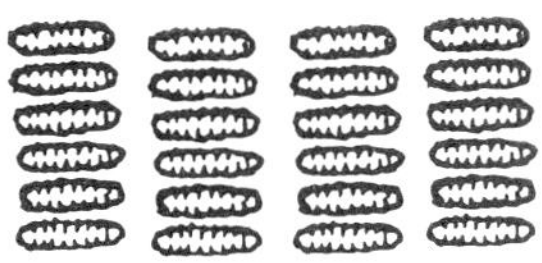

Six rows of corn, with *four* ears of corn in each row!

Trembling with excitement, he counted the ears of corn one by one. There were 24. He added 6 + 6 + 6 + 6. The answer was 24. He added 4 + 4 + 4 + 4 + 4 + 4. The answer was 24. "But I don't have to count any more," he said. "And I don't have to add any more. Whenever I have corn laid out like that, six ears one way, four ears the other way, I'll *remember* I have twenty-four ears of corn." He had discovered multiplication.

He had also discovered that when you multiply the same numbers, you always get the same answer. That is, $6 \times 4 = 4 \times 6$. It doesn't matter what order you multiply them in.

Of course, just remembering that $6 \times 4 = 24$ didn't help the cook very much. It wasn't often that the Pharaoh had only three friends to dinner. So the cook had to remember $6 \times 23 = 138$ and $6 \times 14 = 84$ and $6 \times 31 = 186$ and all sorts of multiplication rules.

Maybe that's as far as he ever got—remembering. Or maybe one day he remembered *wrong* and didn't cook enough corn. The Pharaoh used to carry a thing called a *flail,* which looked sort of like a whip. He probably gave

the poor cook quite a beating with it, yelling, "Next time, be sure there's enough corn!"

So maybe the cook thought of a way to make sure. There was a little wooden table in the corner of the kitchen. When the cook put out rows of corn on the big table, he would take a kitchen knife and run over and carve the problems and answers in the top of the little table.

He called it his multiplication table.

Carving was hard work. The cook didn't want to carve the whole problem every time. He thought of a way to use some of the numbers over again. The top of the little table began to look like this:

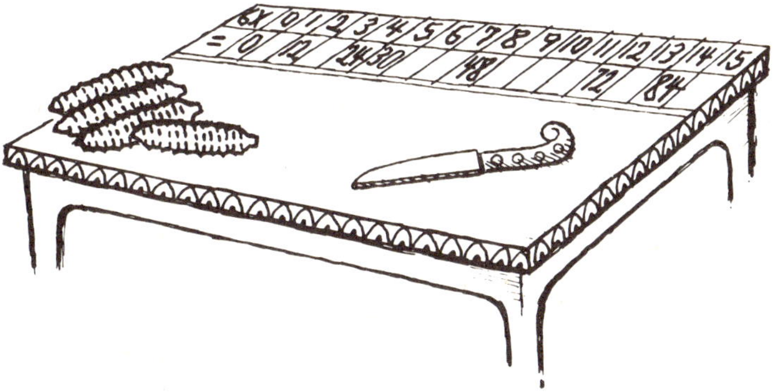

I *told* you he was a lazy, clever cook. Since you are *more* clever but *less* lazy than he was, you might want to fill in the places he left out.

(If you do, you might look along the row of answers. Notice the counting-words that are sitting in the doorway-place in each answer. Interesting, isn't it?)

The little table was too small. I'm sure the cook kept adding more and more problems and answers, but the

Pharaoh had too many friends. That's why I think the cook had to make some more discoveries:

Maybe he had just put out the corn for the Pharaoh and four friends who were coming to dinner—five rows with six ears of corn in each—and had just finished saying, "Five by six. Six times five. What does my multiplication table say? Thirty." And maybe the Pharaoh wandered in at that moment and said, "What are we having for supper tonight? Oh, corn. Good. I like corn. Be sure there's enough corn. By the way, old Memnon is in town with his army, and he'll be bringing some of his officers over for supper. That will be another four hundred people at supper. So be sure there's enough corn. But not too much. Don't waste corn, I always say." And he wandered out.

And maybe the cook said to himself: "Oh, that crazy Pharaoh! *Now* he tells me! We'll have four hundred and five people to supper instead of only five. Six corncobs each for four hundred and five people. Six times four hundred and five. Too high for my table. Wait a minute! I don't have to do it that way. The table does have six times five on it. Thirty. That will take care of that crazy Pharaoh and his friends. All I have to do is *add* enough corn for old Memnon and his officers. That's six times four hundred. I don't know what six times four hundred is. But I know what six times four is. That's carried on the table. Twenty-four. Does that help? No, it doesn't . . . Yes, it does! If I put out six rows with four ears of corn in each row, I have twenty-four ears of corn. Ah, but suppose I get a lot of sacks, and I put one hundred ears of corn in each sack. And suppose I put out six rows with four *sacks* in each row. That means I have six rows with four hundred ears of corn in each row. But the little table says I have twenty-four sacks. And *that* means twenty-four

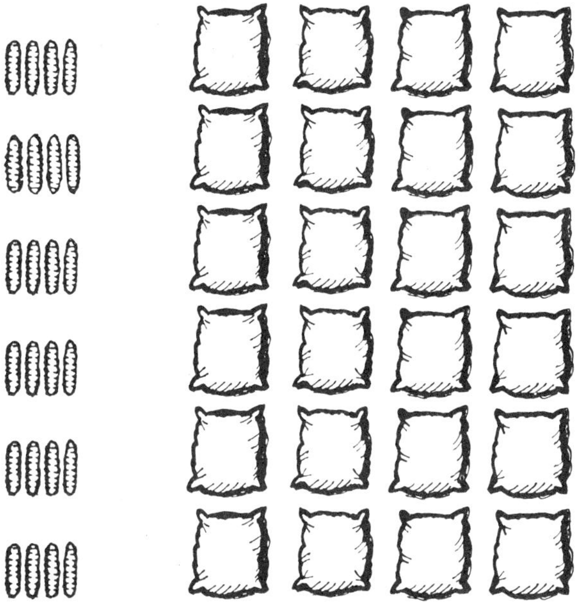

hundred ears of corn. I'm brilliant. I'm absolutely brilliant today . . . I've already put out thirty ears of corn for the Pharaoh and his friends. Now I have to put out twenty-four hundred more for old fat Memnon and his officers. That's twenty-four hundred and thirty . . . I must remember that six times four hundred and five is twenty-four hundred and thirty. I wish I had room on the table."

The cook had discovered two great facts about multiplication. This is the first fact:

Take any two numbers—let's say 4 and 3. Take a third number, any number—let's say 5. Then you multiply the first number by the third—$4 \times 5 = 20$. And you multiply the second number by the third—$3 \times 5 = 15$. Then you *add* the two *multiplication* answers—$20 + 15 = 35$. Now start over and do it a different way. Take those first two numbers and add them together—$4 + 3 = 7$. Now take that third number and *multiply* it by the *addition* answer—$5 \times 7 = 35$. You get the same thing.

Of course, you can see this very easily if you look at two pictures:

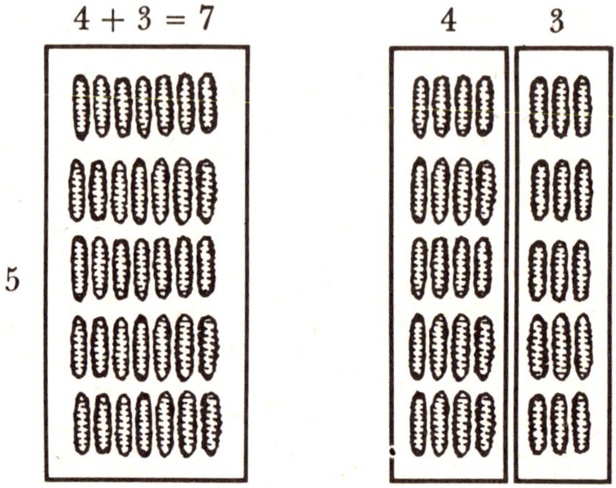

$$\begin{array}{r} 7 \\ \times 5 \\ \hline 35 \end{array} \qquad \begin{array}{r} 4 \\ \times 5 \\ \hline 20 \end{array} \quad \begin{array}{r} 3 \\ \times 5 \\ \hline 15 \end{array}$$

$$\begin{array}{r} 20 \\ +15 \\ \hline 35 \end{array}$$

$(4 + 3) \times 5 = 35$

$5 \times 7 = 35$ $\qquad$ $15 + 20 = 35$

Even though it looks simple, this fact is tremendously useful. One of the things you can do with it is to make big, hard multiplication problems into little, easy multiplication problems. The Pharaoh's cook discovered that, too. He had to multiply 405×6. The poor fellow had always had to put out rows and rows of corn to find the answers to his multiplication problems. Even if he had room to carve it on the little multiplication table, it was always hard the first time. Now he saw how he could get the answer to 405 × 6 without doing so much work. He could *break up* 405 into two numbers.

He knew that 400 + 5 = 405. So he picked 400 and 5. Of course, 399 + 6 = 405, too. And 299 + 106 = 405. There are lots and lots of ways to break up 405. The cook picked 400 and 5 because it was the easiest way. It was the easiest way because this way he didn't have to change any of the counting-names. The 4 stayed a 4. The 5 stayed a 5. I *told* you he was a lazy, clever cook, didn't I?

So now he knew that instead of doing this problem

$$\begin{array}{r} 405 \\ \times 6 \\ \hline \end{array}$$

he could do these two multiplication problems

$$\begin{array}{r} 400 \\ \times 6 \\ \hline \end{array} \qquad \begin{array}{r} 5 \\ \times 6 \\ \hline \end{array}$$

and add the answers.

Well, that little problem over on the right is easy. (It was carved on the table, anyway.)

$$\begin{array}{r} 5 \\ \times 6 \\ \hline 30 \end{array}$$

But the other problem is still hard. Luckily the cook had discovered another fact about multiplication.

You remember that he said to himself: "Suppose I get a lot of sacks, and I put one hundred ears of corn in each sack. And suppose I put out six rows with four sacks in each row. That means I have six rows with four *hundred* ears of corn in each row. But I have twenty-four sacks. And that means twenty-four *hundred* ears of corn."

That was his second new fact about multiplication. It is just as important as the first one. Suppose you have *three* numbers, any three—let's say 3, 4 and 5. And suppose you multiply any two of them—let's say $3 \times 4 = 12$. And then you multiply the answer by the *other* number —that would be $12 \times 5 = 60$. Now start over again. This time you start with 4 and 5—$4 \times 5 = 20$. You multiply the answer by 3—$20 \times 3 = 60$. Same number as before. It doesn't matter which two numbers you multiply first.

You can see this easily enough. Look at this picture:

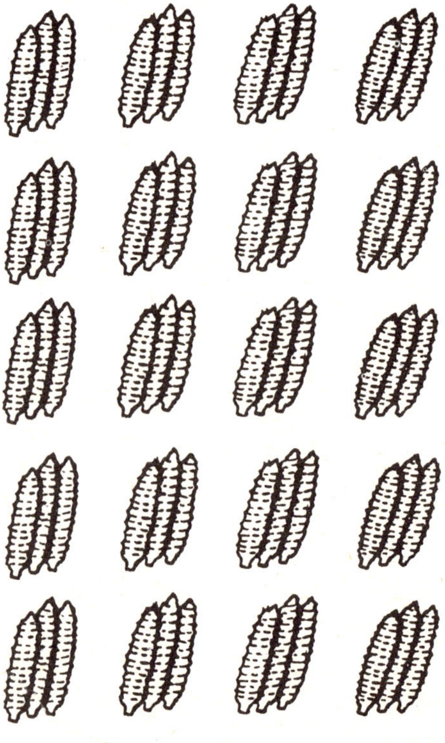

There are 5 rows with 4 heaps in each row and with 3 ears of corn in each heap. There are 60 ears of corn. You can count those 60 ears of corn by counting all the ones at the *bottom* of the heaps ($4 \times 5 = 20$) and then saying that there are 20 middle ones and 20 top ones ($3 \times 20 = 60$). Or you can count all the ears of corn in one row ($3 \times 4 = 12$) and say that there are 5 of these rows ($12 \times 5 = 60$). Or you can count the ears in the *first* heaps of the rows ($3 \times 5 = 15$) and say that there are 4 heaps in each row ($4 \times 15 = 60$).

So the problem

$$\begin{array}{r} 400 \\ \times 6 \\ \hline \end{array}$$

is really $100 \times 4 \times 6$. We can do it

$$\begin{array}{r} 100 \\ \times 4 \\ \hline 400 \\ \times 6 \\ \hline \end{array}$$

but that leaves us with a problem that is a bit hard. We can also do it

$$\begin{array}{r} 4 \\ \times 6 \\ \hline 24 \\ \times 100 \\ \hline \end{array}$$

and that leaves us with an easy problem, because 100 times any number is *that number of hundreds.* (Think about it. Read page 62 and page 69. You'll see why.) So now the cook has

$$
\begin{array}{rcrl}
4 & & & \\
\times 6 & & & \\
\hline
24 & & 5 & \\
\times 100 & & \times 6 & \\
\hline
2400 & + & 30 & = 2430
\end{array}
$$

He has 2430 ears of corn to boil. Let's leave him alone.

I don't really know if it *was* an Egyptian cook who discovered and invented all those things. It could have been a cave man. Or it could have been one of the Emperor of China's tax collectors. No one knows.

(In telling this story, I've used our way of writing down counting-names. That was wrong. But I didn't know what else to do.)

The multiplication table was a very good invention. Sooner or later, somebody learned how to write it so it gave answers to more problems, not just 6-times-a-number problems.

It looked something like the table on the next page.

It's easy to use this multiplication table. You probably know how, but I'll remind you: Suppose you are multiplying 3 × 4. You go down the list of names of numbers *under* the ×, until you come to 3. You put your left index finger on that. You go along the row of names of numbers *next to* the × until you come to 4. You put your right index finger on that. Then you do two things at once. You move your left index finger across—be careful not to let it wander up or down into another row. And you move your right index finger straight down—be careful not to let it wander to the right or left into another list. Your fingers ought to meet at 12. That's your answer. Since $3 \times 4 = 4 \times 3$, you ought to get the same answer if you put your left index finger on 4 and move it across, while you put your right index finger on 3 and move it down, until they meet . . . And you *do* get 12.

×	0	1	2	3	4	5	6	7	8	9	10
0	0	0	0	0	0		0				0
1	0	1	2	3	4					9	10
2	0	2	4		8	10	12	14	16	18	20
3	0	3		9	12	15		21			
4	0	4	8	12		20	24				
5			10	15	20	25	30	35			
6	0		12		24	30			48		
7			14	21		35		49			
8			16				48				
9		9	18								
10	0	10	20								

I haven't put in all the answers. I thought you'd like to do it—on your own piece of paper, of course.

While you're doing it, you'll begin to notice some interesting things. For instance, in the row next to 10, what do you see? Is there an easy way to write out the list under 5 without really thinking very hard?

I've darkened some of the squares. Those answers are special answers. You'll soon see why—or perhaps you already see.

The number whose name is Zero or 0 is a very strange number. You can add it to another number, and the other number doesn't change.

$$1 + 0 = 1$$

$$2 + 0 = 2$$

$$3 + 0 = 3$$

$$4 + 0 = 4$$

It looks as if Zero is a very *weak* number.

But just try it in multiplication. (Look at the table.)

$$1 \times 0 = 0$$

$$2 \times 0 = 0$$

$$3 \times 0 = 0$$

$$4 \times 0 = 0$$

It's not weak. It's so strong that it just blows away the other numbers.

The number whose name is One or 1 is also a strange number. In adding, it looks very useful.

$$0 + 1 = 1$$

$$1 + 1 = 2$$

$$2 + 1 = 3$$

$$3 + 1 = 4$$

$$4 + 1 = 5$$

But in multiplication it isn't useful at all. (Look at the table.)

$$1 \times 1 = 1$$

$$2 \times 1 = 2$$

$$3 \times 1 = 3$$

$$4 \times 1 = 4$$

It just doesn't seem to do any work.

We have just discovered some strange facts about adding and multiplying with 0 and 1. Now let's clench our fists. We haven't got fingers. We have hoofs. We're billy goats.

We billy goats use the pictures 0 and 1 to make the names of all our numbers. Are those strange facts *good* for us or *bad* for us? We'd better see if we're going to have trouble adding and multiplying.

We'll begin by writing down some things we know about addition, using billy goat names:

FIRST FACT: $0 + 0 = 0$

SECOND FACT: $0 + 1 = 1$

THIRD FACT: $1 + 1 = 10$

That's all we can say about adding numbers that have only *one place* in their names.

Wouldn't it be nice if that were *all* we ever had to remember about addition? Just think: those poor *people* who speak people language have about a hundred different facts to remember—like $3 + 4 = 7$, and $1 + 9 = 10$, and $4 + 7 = 11$.

Well, let's investigate or experiment. Let's see if those three facts about billy goat addition will work in *any* place, not just the doorway-place.

We'll set up an addition problem with 0 + 0 in one or two places, 0 + 1 in one or two places, and 1 + 1 in one or two places. Of course we'll add *place by place*. That is, we'll be careful to add the doorway-place of one number to the doorway-place of the other number; we'll add the place-worth-two to the place-worth-two; we'll add the place-worth-four to the place-worth-four; and so on.

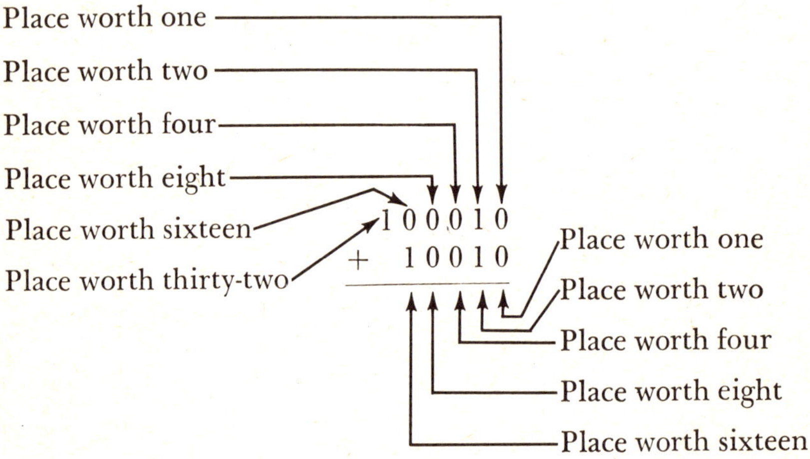

And we'll add *as if* those three facts were true:

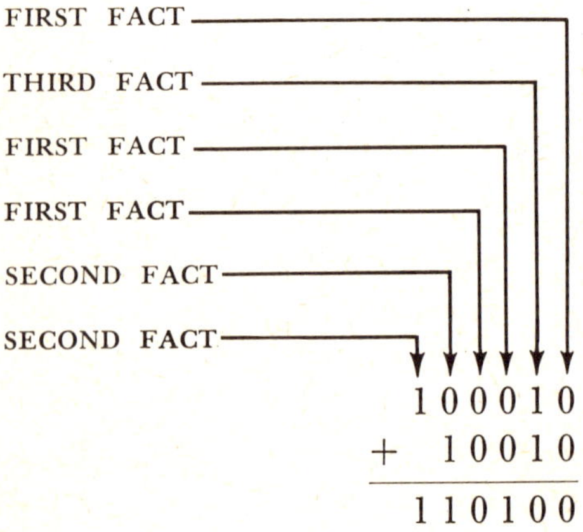

We have an easy way of finding out if we got the right answer. We look in the lists you made on page 63 and find the people names of the two numbers we have added. Then we add them the way people do. Then we look up our people answer in your lists and see what the billy goat answer should be . . .

And it *is* the answer we got.

And that means that we billy goats *don't* have to remember a hundred facts about addition. We have to remember only three.

We're still billy goats.

We're going to write down what we know about multiplying:

$$0 \times 0 = 0$$

$$0 \times 1 = 0$$

$$1 \times 1 = 1$$

Is this *all* there is to know? *People* (those poor silly animals!) have to know a hundred facts about multiplication—like $5 \times 3 = 15$ and $6 \times 7 = 42$ and $9 \times 9 = 81$. Maybe we billy goats are luckier.

Let's investigate some more. Suppose we have a row of corncobs and a row of counting-word-places with nothing in them:

First of all, what happens when we multiply 1 times a bigger number? (We could peek at the people's multiplication table which you made on page 75. That would tell us. After all, billy goat numbers are the same as people numbers—it's just that their *names* are different. But peeking at the table isn't as much fun as investigating or experimenting.) Here is a problem: 1 × 101 = ?

What does 1 × 101 mean?

Well, we know that 3 × 4 means 3 rows with 4 things in each row—darn it, I was using people's counting-names! In our own billy goat counting-names, 11 × 100 means 11 rows with 100 things in each row.

So 1 × 101 must mean 1 row with 101 things in it:

How many things are there? Why, 101, of course!

So we know that 1 times a bigger number is simply that same old bigger number.

Now, for our next experiment, let's find out what happens when we multiply some number by a 10 or 100 or 1000 or 10000. What happens when we multiply 10 × 101? We'll set up a row of counting-word places with nothing in them, and we'll set up 10 rows with 101 corncobs in each of them:

Let's take the first corncob from each row and put *both* of them into the row of counting-places *at the same time.* Here they come!

They get to the doorway. They push and shove and squeeze in together. Each of them turns into a 1. But we know what happens when a 1 and another 1 try to stand in the same place. They both go on to the next place, and they turn into a single 1:

We can see right away what is happening: when two Ones enter the counting-places at the same time, they go right past the doorway-place and into the place-worth-two. And when this has happened 101 times, we'll have 1010 in the counting-places. If you don't believe me, just count the corncobs in these 10 rows with 101 corncobs in each row:

Let's think about 100 × 101. That means we have 100 rows with 101 corncobs in each row:

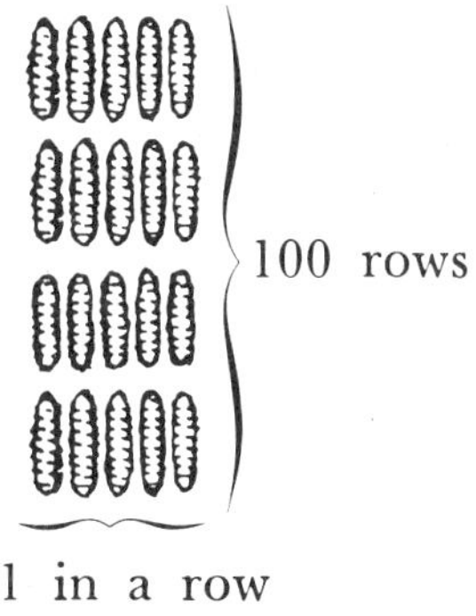

Suppose we took the first corncob from each row. And suppose we tried to squeeze all 4 of them—excuse me, all 100 of them—into a row of counting-places at the same time. What would happen? Why, they'd go right past the doorway-place and right past the place-worth-two and they'd go straight to the place-worth-four. So we'd end up with 10100. If you don't believe me, count those corncobs.

So now we know what happens when we multiply any number by a number whose name is 1 with 0 or 00 or 000 or 0000 after it. In 10, the 1 is one place to the left of the doorway-place. So we take all the words in the number's counting-name and we move them one place to the left:

$$10 \times 111 = 1110$$

In 100, the 1 is two places to the left of the doorway-place, so we move all the words two places to the left:

$$100 \times 111 = 11100$$

In 1000, the 1 is three places to the left of the doorway-place, so we move everything three places to the left:

$$1000 \times 111 = 111000$$

That's an easy rule.

Like the Pharaoh's cook, we billy goats have learned to break up hard multiplication problems into easy multiplication problems. Since $10 + 1 = 11$, then we can break up the problem

$$\begin{array}{r} 101 \\ \times 11 \\ \hline \end{array}$$

into two problems:

$$\begin{array}{r} 101 \\ \times 10 \\ \hline \end{array} \quad \text{and} \quad \begin{array}{r} 101 \\ \times 1 \\ \hline \end{array}$$

Both of these are as easy as pie:

$$\begin{array}{r} 101 \\ \times 10 \\ \hline 1010 \end{array} \quad \text{and} \quad \begin{array}{r} 101 \\ \times 1 \\ \hline 101 \end{array}$$

We add the answers:

$$\begin{array}{r} 1010 \\ +101 \\ \hline 1111 \end{array}$$

So $11 \times 101 = 1111$.

But we billy goats don't like to spread our work over the page like that. We're neat. We write it out this way:

$$\left\{\begin{array}{r} 101 \\ \times 11 \\ \hline 101 \\ +1010 \\ \hline 1111 \end{array}\right\} \quad \text{or} \quad \left\{\begin{array}{r} 11 \\ \times 101 \\ \hline 11 \\ +1100 \\ \hline 1111 \end{array}\right\}$$

When it comes to adding and multiplying, we billy goats have a *much* easier life than people do.

Straighten your fingers. We're *people* again.

AS soon as people found out about addition, they tried to answer all sorts of questions with it. One sort of question went like this: *If I want to eat five ears of corn for supper and I have three of them already, how many more ears of corn do I need?*

People could see that this was really the same as asking *What number must I add to 3 to get 5?*

You can imagine some fellow saying very excitedly, "The answer is Three! I just know it is!" So they would add 3 and 3 and most of them would get 6.

"No," they would say sadly, "too big."

"Well, then, try One. That's smaller," some other fellow would say. So they would add 3 and 1 and get 4.

"Too small," they would say. "What shall we do?"

At last some very clever fellow would say, "Why don't we use a number that's bigger than One and smaller than Three?"

"A fine idea!" they would all say. "Uh–just which number did you have in mind?"

The clever one would think hard for a while and say "Two." And 2 would work.

But that way of answering this kind of question was really too slow and hard when the numbers were big. Somebody had to invent a better way. And somebody did. I don't know who it was. Probably it was a lot of different people, in a lot of different places. I like to think that in one place it happened like this:

Once upon a time, in the mysterious country called China, there lived an old farmer named Ching Wu. Ching Wu had a long thin beard. He also had a short thick

wife. They had seven sons and seven daughters.

The seven sons went away and got married. The seven daughters got married and went away.

"Have you noticed," said Ching Wu to his wife one day, "that it's very *quiet* around here?"

"Yes," said the old lady happily.

A few months later, Ching Wu said to his wife, "Isn't it *quiet* around here?"

"Yes," said the old lady sadly.

A few months later, Ching Wu said to his wife, "I find it *quiet* around here, don't you?"

"Yes," said the old lady, and burst into tears.

"I have an idea," said Ching Wu. "Let's invite all the children to come and visit us."

"Yes," said the old lady, and she stopped crying.

So all the children came to celebrate the Chinese New Year, and the daughters brought their husbands, and the sons brought their wives.

When you celebrate the Chinese New Year, you do it *loudly,* with *firecrackers.* Ching Wu took five geese to market and bought a big box full of big firecrackers, and after a big dinner Ching Wu and his wife and the sons and the daughters-in-law and the daughters and the sons-in-law each took a firecracker out of the box and they all set off their firecrackers at the same time. *Bang!*

The next day, when all the sons and daughters and daughters-in-law and sons-in-law had gone home, Ching Wu said to his wife, "Doesn't it seem *quiet* around here?"

"Yes," said the old lady happily.

Ching Wu looked in the box of firecrackers. There were twenty left. "Let me see," said Ching Wu. "Feng Yee the firecracker-maker said there were fifty in the box. Our sons used seven. Our daughters used seven. That's fourteen. Our sons' wives used seven. That's twenty-one. Our daughters' husbands used seven. That's twenty-eight. And there are twenty left in the box. That's forty-eight. Feng Yee said there were fifty. He robbed me!"

"Just a minute," said his wife.

Ching Wu did not listen to her. He said, "Feng Yee was supposed to give me ten firecrackers for every goose. I gave him five geese. Five times ten is fifty. He robbed me!"

"Just a minute," said the old lady.

"Luckily," said Ching Wu, not listening to her, "one

of those geese was very skinny. So Feng Yee didn't get the better of me after all."

"Just a minute," said the old lady. "Did you say there were twenty-eight people at the party?"

"Yes," said Ching Wu.

"You forgot two people," said his wife.

"Who?"

"Ching Wu and his wife," said the old lady.

"Why, so I did! So I did!" said Ching Wu, and laughed heartily. "So I did! Well," he said, "now that I think about it, that skinny goose was really quite fat."

A few months later, Ching Wu said to his wife, "It's still pretty *quiet* around here, don't you think?"

"Yes," said the old lady, and she began to weep.

So the next New Year's Day, all the sons and their wives and the daughters and their husbands came back for another party. This time some of them brought some new visitors—babies. There were four baby boys and five baby girls.

"Shall we let our grandchildren set off firecrackers?" Ching Wu asked his wife.

"Yes," said the old lady, "but *really* their parents will do it for them."

So after dinner, Ching Wu brought out a huge box of firecrackers, which he had bought from Feng Yee for six geese. He gave one to each son, daughter, daughter-in-law, son-in-law and grandchild. He took one and his wife took one.

Bang!!

The next day, all the visitors went home.

"At last it's *quiet* around here," said Ching Wu to his wife.

"Yes," said the old lady with a smile.

"Let's see how many firecrackers we have left. This year Feng Yee sold me six geese worth, at ten for a goose. That's sixty firecrackers. There were seven sons. And seven daughters-in-law. That's fourteen. And seven daughters. That's twenty-one. And seven sons-in-law. That's twenty-eight. And four grandsons. That's thirty-two. I'm very good at this adding. And five granddaughters. That's thirty-seven. And Ching Wu and his little fat wife. That's thirty-nine. So we ought to have . . . we ought to have . . . well, we had sixty firecrackers, and we used thirty-nine, so we ought to have . . ."

"Why don't you look in the box?" asked the old lady.

"I guess I'll have to," said Ching Wu. "But I *shouldn't* have to. If I have sixty firecrackers and I use up thirty-nine, I ought to have . . . well, there ought to be some number left. And if I add that number to thirty-nine, I ought to get sixty. And there's only one number that I could add to thirty-nine to get sixty. So why don't I know what it is?"

"If you look in the box, you'll know what it is," said the old lady.

Ching Wu looked in the box. "One, two, three, . . . bzzz, bzzz, bzzz . . . nineteen, twenty, twenty-one," he counted. "Thirty-nine and twenty-one. That's thirty-nine and one and twenty. That's forty and twenty. That's sixty. So, the number I wanted was twenty-one."

"I *told* you to look in the box," said the old lady.

A few months later, when Ching Wu happened to ask his wife if it seemed a little *quiet* around there, the old lady surprised him by starting to cry. So they invited their children and grandchildren for a New Year's party. Ching Wu took five geese to market and came home with a box of firecrackers. And this time, all the sons and their wives arrived with babies. And some came with two babies. And all the daughters and their husbands arrived with babies too. Some came with two babies. And one daughter and son-in-law arrived with *three* babies. (Two of those were twins.)

Ching Wu rushed off to the market with five more geese and came back with another box of Feng Yee's best firecrackers.

Big, big dinner.

Bang!!!

Next day. "Goodbye! Goodbye, Papa! Goodbye! Goodbye!" The visitors went away.

"Aren't you glad," said Ching Wu to his wife, "that now we have some *quiet* around here?"

"Yes." Smile.

"Now," said Ching Wu, "let's see. Seven sons. Seven daughters-in-law. Fourteen. Seven daughters. Twenty-one. Seven sons-in-law. Twenty-eight. Eleven grandsons. That's—that's thirty-nine."

"Just a minute," said the old lady.

Ching Wu didn't listen.

"Ten granddaughters. Forty-nine. And Ching Wu and his nice fat wife. That's fifty-one."

"No," said the old lady.

"No?" said Ching Wu, surprised.

"No. *Twelve* grandsons. Not eleven," said the old lady.

"Eleven," said Ching Wu. "There were Tai-Kwee's boy, Mei-Ling's boy—"

"Mei-Ling had twins," said the old lady.

"No, it was Fah-Lo who had twins," said Ching Wu.

"Mei-Ling," said the old lady.

"Anyway, there were eleven," said Ching Wu.

"Twelve."

"I can look in the boxes," said Ching Wu.

"What good will that do?" asked the old lady.

"I took five geese to market and then five more geese. That's ten geese. I got ten firecrackers for each goose. That's one hundred firecrackers. If there were eleven grandsons, there were fifty-one people at the party, so fifty-one firecrackers got used. If there were twelve—"

"There were twelve," said the old lady.

"*If* there were twelve grandsons, there were fifty-*two* people at the party, and fifty-*two* firecrackers got used. And that means . . ."

"Yes?" said the old lady.

"Well, it means . . ."

"Yes?" said the old lady.

"Well, there's a number that . . . well, if I added it to fifty-one, I'd get one hundred. There's only one number like that. And then if I looked in the box, and counted the firecrackers, and there were *that number* . . . well, the firecrackers we used and the firecrackers we didn't use ought to add up to one hundred . . . so if there were *that number* of firecrackers we didn't use, then there must have been fifty-one we did use."

"What is *that number?*" asked the old lady.

"That's what I don't know," said Ching Wu sadly. He thought for a moment. "I had one hundred firecrackers. I took fifty-one away."

"Fifty-two," said the old lady.

"Well, *if*—I say *if*—I took fifty-one away from one hundred, how many would be left?"

"That number?" asked the old lady, hopefully.

"That number," said Ching Wu. "Ha *ha!* I know what to do! I had two boxes of firecrackers. There were fifty in each box. If I used up fifty-one firecrackers, I used up a

whole box, and I used just one firecracker from the other box. If I take one firecracker away from fifty firecrackers, how many are left?" He thought hard. "Forty-nine!" he said at last. "So if there were fifty-one people at the party, there are forty-nine firecrackers in this box. And if there are forty-nine firecrackers in this box, there were fifty-one people at the party. Ha *ha!*"

Ching Wu counted the firecrackers.

"How many did you find?" asked the old lady.

"Wait a minute," said Ching Wu, looking in the box.

"Are there forty-nine firecrackers?" asked the old lady.

"No," said Ching Wu. "There are . . . well, there seem to be only forty-eight firecrackers."

"What does that mean?" asked the old lady.

"I—I'm not sure," said Ching Wu, "but I think . . . well, if there is one *less* firecracker *here,* then there was one *more* firecracker used at the *party*. There must have been fifty-two people at the party."

"I thought so," said the old lady. "We do have twelve grandsons."

"We must celebrate the birth of our twelfth grandson," said Ching Wu happily. "Have a firecracker."

As soon as Ching Wu (and lots of other people) had invented subtraction, people began to ask a new question:

Suppose I have 39 things—oh, let's say they're corncobs. And suppose I subtract 3 corncobs. And suppose I subtract 3 more corncobs. And 3 more. And suppose I keep doing this. *How many times can I subtract 3 from 39 before the 39 is all used up?*

Let's try it:

$39 - 3 = 36$	That's once.
$36 - 3 = 33$	That's twice.
$33 - 3 = 30$	That's three times.
$30 - 3 = 27$	That's four times.
$27 - 3 = 24$	That's five times.
$24 - 3 = 21$	That's six times.
$21 - 3 = 18$	That's seven times.
$18 - 3 = 15$	That's eight times.
$15 - 3 = 12$	That's nine times.
$12 - 3 = 9$	That's ten times.
$9 - 3 = 6$	That's eleven times.
$6 - 3 = 3$	That's twelve times.
$3 - 3 = 0$	That's thirteen times.

The answer is 13.

But this takes much too much work. It was just too hard for simple, busy men—like soldiers. Yet soldiers had to answer this kind of question all the time.

I'm sure that Achilles and Odysseus and the other mighty warriors of ancient Greece had a lot of trouble

with this question when they were fighting their famous battles outside the great city of Troy.

Perhaps one day Achilles came marching back from a battle, leading 23 of his fierce soldiers. They had won, and they were carrying armloads of swords and spears they had taken from the Trojans they had beaten. The same day, Odysseus came marching back with 18 of *his* soldiers, and *they* had won, and *they* were carrying armloads of spears and bows they had taken from the Trojans *they* had beaten.

"Ah, good afternoon, mighty Achilles," said Odysseus politely. "And I see that it *has* been a good afternoon."

"Ah, wise Odysseus," said Achilles. "Yes, we *have* picked up a few nice little toys today. And such good fun we had, too! Such blood and yelling! It has been a *good* afternoon. I hope you had the same."

"Not bad, not bad," said Odysseus. "As you see, we have not wasted our time. All right, men. Companeeee, atten-SHUN! Forwaaard, MARCH! *One* two three four, *one* two three four . . ."

"Companeeee," Achilles shouted to his men, "atten-SHUN! Forwaaard, MARCH! *One* two—hm—er—*left* right, *left* right, *left* right . . ."

And both companies marched into the Greek camp.

When Achilles and his men got to their tents, they threw all the swords in one pile and all the spears in another. Then they started to count them. This was very hard. One soldier counted the swords and said there were 68. Another said there were 71. Another soldier counted the spears and said there were 127. Another said there were 133. There was a lot of shouting and fist-shaking, and then the soldiers woke up Achilles and asked him to count the swords and spears *right*.

Achilles, who was very stupid, did not know how to count. So he said, "How dare you wake me up! I'm a prince! Do you think princes worry about things like numbers?" And he went back to sleep.

There was some more shouting and fist-shaking and then a soldier said, "We'll all line up. And we'll march past the swords. And as we go past, each of us will take a sword. Then we'll go and put our swords in our tents. Then we'll line up again and march past again, and each will take another sword. And we'll put those in our tents. And we'll keep doing this till all the swords are gone."

Then all the soldiers tried to get at the front of the line, because each of them said to himself, "Maybe the last time we march past, there won't be enough swords left for everybody. I'll go first, so I'll be sure of getting one."

After more shouting and fist-shaking *and* pushing, a soldier said, "Wait a minute! Ouch! Stop pushing! I have an idea. The last time we march past the pile, if there aren't enough swords left for everybody, the ones that do get swords won't take them to their tents. We'll take them to Achilles, and he can have them."

While this was going on, Odysseus and his men had marched to their tents and made a pile of spears and a pile of bows.

"There are 110 spears here," said Odysseus, who could count. "There are 18 of you men. And there's one of me. That's 19 of us. I want each of us to get the same number of spears. But how many is that? Let me think." He thought. "I want you to take all these 110 spears and lay them out in rows. There should be 19 in each row."

The soldiers laid the spears out:

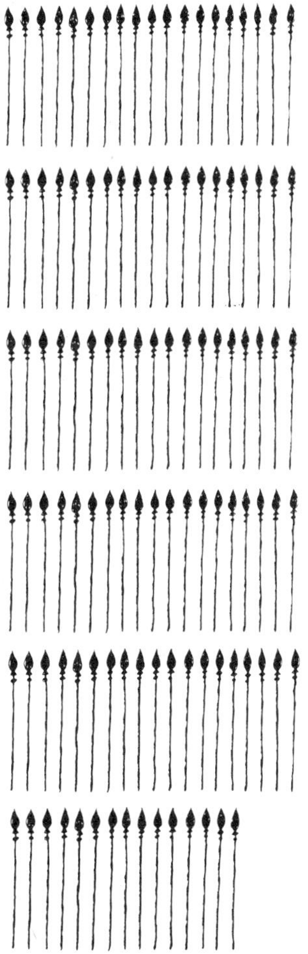

"Well," said Odysseus, "there are 5 whole rows with 19 spears in them, so each of us will get 5 spears. And there are 15 spears left over, so I'll take those."

"Why should you get 5 spears like us *and also* get 15 spears more?" asked a soldier.

"Because I'm a king," said Odysseus.

"Oh!" said the soldier. "I knew there was some reason."

"Now," said Odysseus, "there are 84 bows here. Put them in rows of 19."

The soldiers did.

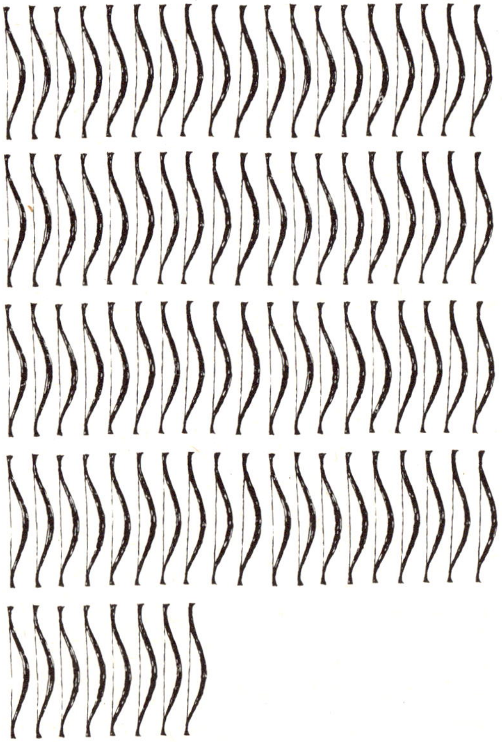

"There are 4 rows, and 8 bows left over," said Odysseus. "Let's see if that's right. Four times nineteen . . . bzzz

bzzz . . . six, and three to the tens place . . . bzzz bzzz . . . four ones is four, and three is seven . . . bzzz bzzz . . . makes seventy-six. Seventy-six and eight . . . bzzz bzzz . . . one to the tens place . . . eighty-four. That's right, 84 bows. So we'll each take 4 bows, and I'll take the 8 bows that are left over. Because I'm a king. Companeeee, atten-SHUN! DIS-miss!"

While Odysseus' soldiers were going off to their tents, each carrying 5 spears and 4 bows, Achilles' soldiers were still rushing around, trying to divide up the pile of swords. The soldiers didn't know it, but there were 70 swords, and after subtracting 23 from 70 three times by marching around and rushing back and forth, the soldiers saw that there were three swords for each of them and one left for Achilles. $3 \times 23 = 69$. $69 + 1 = 70$.

While Odysseus' men were smacking their lips over supper, Achilles' men were marching back and forth and rushing around and sweating and panting, dividing the pile of spears. (They didn't know it, but there were 125 spears in the pile.) At last, when they were so tired and out of breath that they could hardly move, they discovered that they could each have 5 spears, and Achilles could have 10. By this time, Odysseus' men were snoring happily in their tents.

You, who are even wiser than Odysseus, must already have noticed two important facts about subtraction and division.

Subtracting is just adding, only it's the other way around. You can say $4 + 3 = 7$. You can say $7 - 3 = 4$. You are really saying the same thing. You can ask $4 +$ what number? $= 7$. You can ask $7 - 4 =$ what number? You are really asking the same thing.

Dividing is just multiplying, only it's the other way around. You can say $4 \times 3 = 12$. You can say $12 \div 3 = 4$. You are really saying the same thing. You can ask $4 \times$ what number? $= 12$. You can ask $12 \div 4 =$ what number? You are really asking the same thing.

But you must also have noticed that one of the important facts about addition and multiplication simply doesn't work with other-way-around addition and other-way-around multiplication.

You remember from page 64 that when you are adding numbers, it doesn't matter what order you add them in:

$$3 + 4 = 7 \qquad 4 + 3 = 7$$

The same is true with multiplication. You remember page 66. If you are multiplying numbers, it doesn't matter what order you multiply them in:

$$3 \times 4 = 12 \qquad 4 \times 3 = 12$$

But that isn't true with subtraction. With subtraction, it certainly *does* matter what order you put the numbers in: $4 - 3 = 1$. But $3 - 4 =$ something that *isn't* 1.

And when you are dividing, the order matters too: $12 \div 4 = 3$. But $4 \div 12 =$ something that isn't 3.

In lots of other ways, though, subtraction *is* like addition, and division *is* like multiplication.

There is one very important fact—a very very powerful fact—about division:

Suppose you add two numbers together, and divide the addition answer by a third number—you will end up with a certain number.

Now suppose you take those first two numbers and you divide each of them separately by the third number, and suppose you add those two division answers together—you will end up with the same number as you did before.

Suppose I add 12 and 9. $12 + 9 = 21$. Now I divide that addition answer by 3. $21 \div 3 = 7$.

Now I'll start over again with 12 and 9. Suppose I divide 12 by 3. $12 \div 3 = 4$. And I divide 9 by 3. $9 \div 3 = 3$. Now I add the division answers. $4 + 3 = 7$.

I end up with the same number, you see. This is tremendously useful. You can use it to break up big hard problems into little easy problems.

Suppose you have the number 396. You want to divide it by 3. I don't know why—you just do, that's all. If you divided 396 by 3 the way Achilles' men did—by subtracting 3 over and over and over again—it would take a long time. Even if you did it the way Odysseus did—by drawing 396 lines in rows with 3 lines in each row—it would be hard. Luckily, you know that

$$396 = 300 + 90 + 6$$

In order to do $396 \div 3$, you can do $300 \div 3$ and $90 \div 3$ and $6 \div 3$ and then add those answers together.

That last little problem, $6 \div 3$, is easy: $2 \times 3 = 6$. So $6 \div 3 = 2$.

Next: $90 \div 3 =$ what number? That's hard.

Let's say it another way—$3 \times$ what number? $= 90$. That's harder.

But wait a minute. Think about this the way William Gruff or the Pharaoh's cook would think about it. Think of 90 corncobs. And think of putting them into 3 rows, with the same number of corncobs in each row—how many will you put in each row? That's still hard.

Think of some sacks. And think of putting 10 corncobs in each sack. You have 90 corncobs. How many sacks will you use? $9 \times 10 = 90$. $90 \div 10 = 9$. You'll use 9 sacks.

If you have 9 sacks of corncobs, and put them in 3 rows, how many sacks will you have in each row? $3 \times 3 = 9$. $9 \div 3 = 3$. You'll have 3 sacks in each row. There are 10 corncobs in each sack. $3 \times 10 = 30$. So you'll have 30 corncobs in each row.

So $30 \times 3 = 90$. So $90 \div 3 = 30$. That's easy.

And $300 \div 3 =$ what number? Or you can ask: $3 \times$ what number? $= 300$. That's *very* easy. $3 \times 100 = 300$. So $300 \div 3 = 100$.

You're almost done.

$$300 \div 3 = 100$$

$$90 \div 3 = 30$$

and $$6 \div 3 = 2$$

You add the division answers together:

$$100 + 30 + 2 = 132$$

So $396 \div 3 = 132$.

I'm going to use a different way of writing down all that dividing:

Instead of $300 \div 3 = 100$, I'll write

$$\begin{array}{r} 100 \\ 3\,\overline{)\,300} \end{array}$$

Instead of $90 \div 3 = 30$, I'll write

$$\begin{array}{r} 30 \\ 3\,\overline{)\;\;90} \end{array}$$

Instead of $6 \div 3 = 2$, I'll write

$$\begin{array}{r} 2 \\ 3\,\overline{)\;\;\;\;6} \end{array}$$

Now look carefully at these six division problems:

$$\begin{array}{ccc} \begin{array}{r} 100 \\ 3\,\overline{)\,300} \end{array} & \begin{array}{r} 30 \\ 3\,\overline{)\,90} \end{array} & \begin{array}{r} 2 \\ 3\,\overline{)\,6} \end{array} \\ \\ \begin{array}{r} 1 \\ 3\,\overline{)\,3} \end{array} & \begin{array}{r} 3 \\ 3\,\overline{)\,9} \end{array} & \begin{array}{r} 2 \\ 3\,\overline{)\,6} \end{array} \end{array}$$

Which look easier, the ones on top or the ones on the bottom?

Surely the ones on the bottom look easier—except for the ones over on the right, which are just the same on the top *and* the bottom.

And it would be easy to change the bottom ones to the top ones, just by putting in a few Zeros. But instead of that, let's squash the three bottom ones together:

$$\begin{array}{r} 132 \\ 3\,\overline{)\,396} \end{array}$$

There you are.

There is one kind of division you cannot do. I don't mean it's too hard. I mean it just can't be done. Ever.

You can never divide a number by 0.

Imagine what would have happened if Achilles' men had tried to divide 70 by 0. They would have marched back and forth past the pile of 70 swords *never picking up any of them.* Even if they had marched past that pile forever, the pile would never have been divided.

Imagine Odysseus trying to put out 110 spears in rows *with no spears in each row.* He could never even have *started* dividing the spears.

We said that $12 \div 4 = 3$ is another way of saying $3 \times 4 = 12$. If we write $12 \div 0 =$ some number, we mean that some number $\times\ 0 = 12$. But that can't be, because we know that when we multiply any number—any number at all—by Zero, the Zero just blows away the other number. Some number $\times\ 0 = 0$. Always.

What do you suppose would happen if we turned billy goat addition around the other way and did billy goat subtraction?

Our first fact about addition, if you remember, was $0 + 0 = 0$. We turn it around and get

FIRST FACT $\qquad 0 - 0 = 0.$

Our second fact about addition was $0 + 1 = 1$. We turn it around and get

SECOND FACT $\qquad 1 - 1 = 0.$

We could have written that second fact about addition $1 + 0 = 1$. Then, when we turned it around, it would be

THIRD FACT $\qquad 1 - 0 = 1.$

Our third fact about addition was $1 + 1 = 10$. We turn it around and get

FOURTH FACT $\qquad 10 - 1 = 1.$

Now let's see if these facts really work. Here's a problem:

$$\begin{array}{r} 110110 \\ -101010 \\ \hline \end{array}$$

$$\begin{array}{r} 110110 \\ -101010 \\ \hline 0 \end{array}$$

We'll start at the right.
FIRST FACT: 0 – 0 = 0.

$$\begin{array}{r} 110110 \\ -101010 \\ \hline 00 \end{array}$$

Twos Place. SECOND FACT: 1 – 1 = 0.

$$\begin{array}{r} 110110 \\ -101010 \\ \hline 100 \end{array}$$

Fours Place. THIRD FACT: 1 – 0 = 1.

$$\begin{array}{r} 110110 \\ -101010 \\ \hline 1100 \end{array}$$

Eights Place. We're going to have to sneak over into the Sixteens Place.
FOURTH FACT: 10 – 1 = 1.

$$\begin{array}{r} 110110 \\ -101010 \\ \hline 01100 \end{array}$$

Sixteens Place. We already used that 1 on top, so there's nothing there.
FIRST FACT again: 0 – 0 = 0.

$$\begin{array}{r} 110110 \\ -101010 \\ \hline 001100 \end{array}$$

Thirty-Twos Place.
SECOND FACT again: 1 – 1 = 0.

Our answer is 001100. Those Zeros on the left-hand end don't count. So our answer is 1100. Let's check it against your lists on page 63.

$$\begin{array}{rr} 110110 = & 54 \\ -101010 = & -42 \\ \hline 1100 & 12 \end{array}$$

The facts work. Once again, the billy goats have an easier kind of arithmetic than the people do.

Now we'll see what happens when we turn billy goat multiplication around the other way and do billy goat division.

Here's a problem:

$$1010101 \div 101 = ?$$

Let's break this up into two problems. We know that $1010101 = 1010000 + 101$. So we can write

$$1010000 \div 101 = ?$$

and

$$101 \div 101 = ?$$

Well, we had an interesting rule in billy goat multiplication. If we wanted to multiply a certain number by 10, all we had to do was stick a 0 on the end of its name and we'd have the answer: $10 \times 101 = 1010$. If we multiplied a number by 100, we stuck 00 on the end of its name: $100 \times 101 = 10100$. If we multiplied a number by 1000, we simply stuck 000 on the end of its name: $1000 \times 101 = 101000$. And if we multiplied a number by 10000, we stuck 0000 on the end of its name: $10000 \times 101 = 1010000$.

But that's one of the things we're looking for. We turn $10000 \times 101 = 1010000$ around:

$$1010000 \div 101 = 10000$$

That leaves

$$101 \div 101 = ?$$

which is easy. $1 \times 101 = 101$. So $101 \div 101 = 1$.

We add our division answers: $10000 + 1 = 10001$. So

$$1010101 \div 101 = 10001$$

If we use your lists on page 63, we see $85 \div 5 = 17$.

Is that right?

It is.

Now that happens to be an easy problem in billy goat division. Some problems in billy goat division are much harder—*almost* as hard as problems in people division.

Now we know quite a lot about billy goat arithmetic. Maybe you are wishing you could ask me, "If billy goat arithmetic is so easy, why don't we use it instead of people arithmetic?"

Sometimes we do.

Almost every day, the newspapers tell us about a scientist who has made a great discovery by using some wonderful machines called "computers." Sometimes they call the machines "giant brains" or "electronic brains."

When our astronauts go out into space, there are "radars" and "radio-telescopes" and all kinds of radio-eyes watching them from laboratories all over the world. And these radio-eyes are attached to huge computers. These computers do the most difficult arithmetic, and they do it so fast that our scientists back on earth know just where the astronaut is even before he knows it himself.

If you have watched television on the evening of Election Day, you have heard men telling you who would win the election *before the voters had even finished voting.* To do this, they used computers.

These computers aren't really "brains" at all. People can do all kinds of things with their brains—they can write poetry, they can make jokes, they can dream dreams. But computers can do only five things: they can count, they can add, they can multiply, they can subtract, and they can divide.

They can count up to a million in a second or two. They can do thousands and thousands and thousands of arithmetic problems in one second. But that's really all they can do.

All they can do? It's quite a lot.

And the counting-names they use are William Gruff's counting-names. And the arithmetic they do is billy goat arithmetic.

A computer is a huge network of magnets and switches and wires and crystals and lights and motors—connected to tape-recorders and typewriters, so that people can tell the machine their problems and get the machine's answers out of it.

Billy goat arithmetic is just right for these enormous arithmetic-machines, because it uses only two counting-names, 0 and 1—or NO and YES, as William Gruff called them. In a computer, all the numbers have to have *electrical names.* Suppose I want to do something with the number which people would call 37. Of course, I could arrange some lights in the right shape:

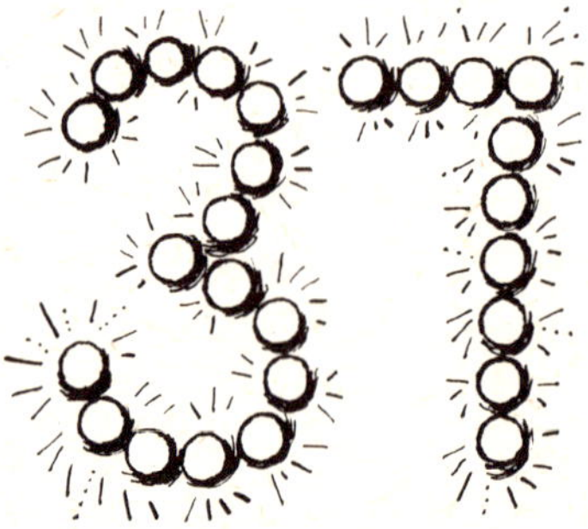

But how would one part of the machine send this number to another part of the machine?

If I used William Gruff's names, however, it would be easy. I could set up a row of lights—or magnets or crystals:

Where William Gruff said YES, I would turn the light on. Where William Gruff said NO, I would turn the light off. The number I have turned on here is 100101, which William Gruff called YES-NO-NO-YES-NO-YES, and which people call 37. Its electrical name is ON-OFF-OFF-ON-OFF-ON.

And by connecting up my wires to the magnets and the crystals and the electric typewriters and the tape-recorders and the switches in just the right way, my machine would "remember" that 1 + 1 = 10 (ON + ON = ON-OFF) and all the other facts of billy goat arithmetic.

The beauty of billy goat arithmetic is that there are so few facts to remember. Just a handful—or a couple of hoofs-full—of facts would be enough for the machine.

And it could steer rockets in space.

And it could help telescopes find stars that were out beyond the Milky Way.

And it could find out how to get atomic energy from sea-water.

And it could find out why tiny germs cause people to die.

It could do arithmetic.